lonely planet

POCKET
ROTTERDAM

Catherine Le Nevez

Contents

Top: Kinderdijk (p132)
Bottom: Delfshaven (p76)

Plan Your Trip 4

Explore Rotterdam 31

Rotterdam Toolkit 143

FROM TOP: PIDJOE/GETTY IMAGES ©, MIHAIULIA/GETTY IMAGES ©

★ Top Experiences

Worth a Trip

The Journey Begins Here

Rotterdam has an energy and spirit that I've not encountered anywhere else in the world. Perhaps it's the resilience of having to rebuild almost entirely from scratch, turning WWII's devastation into an exhilarating and inspirational architectural ride. Or maybe it's sparked by lively rivalry as the country's second-biggest city. Or its unpretentious roots as a working port. (Or a combination of all three.) Seeing seemingly inconceivable ideas come to life like its world-first urban surfing canal sums up why I love Rotterdam. It's a city in perpetual motion, with a determination and irrepressible optimism that's impossible to resist.

Catherine Le Nevez
lonelyplanet.com/authors/catherine-le-nevez
A Lonely Planet author since 2004, contributing to more than 100 guides in some two dozen countries, Catherine has a Doctorate of Creative Arts in Writing and insatiable wanderlust.

Rotterdam cityscape

THE BEST

Architecture Experiences

Rotterdam rose to the challenge after WWII, using the opportunity to create adventurous new buildings alongside structures that survived the bombings, and visionary architects continue to reshape the city's skyline today.

Tour stunning 'glass palace' **Van Nelle Fabriek** (pictured above; p72), an early 20th-century factory and UNESCO World Heritage site.

Look up to see the eye-popping fruit-and-vegetable mural covering the inverted horseshoe of apartments arcing over fabulous **Markthal** (p44) food market; be sure to book a behind-the-scenes tour.

Step inside the show cube of the crazily angled **Blaakse Bos** (p47), Rotterdam's 20th-century yellow-and-white 'forest' of cube houses up on pylons that are a defining feature of Rotterdam's distinctive skyline.

Admire the **Huis Sonneveld** (p36), a wonderfully preserved 1930s family home and example of Functionalism.

Marvel at Europe's first 'skyscraper', the 45m-high Art Nouveau **Witte Huis** (pictured above; p41), completed in 1898 and a rare survivor of the city's prewar architecture.

Right: Blaakse Bos (p47)

FROM LEFT: LEA RAE/SHUTTERSTOCK ©, TRABANTOS/SHUTTERSTOCK ©, QIZAI00/SHUTTERSTOCK ©

THE BEST

Eating Experiences

Taste the flavours of the Netherlands and the world in this multicultural port city and its surrounding towns, cities and coastline, where choices range from traditional treats and inexpensive street snacks to sustainable fine dining.

Dig into a coneful of crispy, fluffy Dutch fries smothered in mayo, peanut or fiery *oorlog* sauce (plus onions) at **Schipper Patat** (p53), a Rotterdam staple.

Take high tea served on hand-painted porcelain at the factory where it's made, 17th-century **Royal Delft** (p105).

Devour sticky syrup-filled *stroopwafels* after watching them being made in the kitchens of cheese-famed Gouda's **Kamphuisen Siroopwafels** (p134).

Choose among global cuisines at the Dutch East India Company (VOC) warehouse Pakhuismeesteren, now housing **Foodhallen Rotterdam** (p92).

Dine on fresh seafood caught by its own fishing fleet at **Simonis aan de Haven** (p128) at Scheveningen's harbour.

Kamphuisen Siroopwafels (p134)

THE BEST

Drinking Experiences

Being served a glass of *bier* (beer), its foam skimmed off by a spatula, is a quintessential Dutch experience, and there are great breweries around town. *Jenever* is another must-try in the distillers district at Schiedam.

Breathe in the scents of barley and grain being malted at the *jenever* (traditional Dutch gin) distillery housing the **Nationaal Jenevermuseum Schiedam** (pictured above; p80) in Schiedam's Dutch Distillers District, home to the world's tallest windmills.

Take a watertaxi from the Katendrecht taproom of **Kaapse Brouwers** (p91) as part of behind-the-scenes tours of its Keilehaven brewery.

Go straight to the source at **Giraffe Coffee Bar & Academy** (p56), which supplies cafes around Rotterdam, runs workshops such as latte art and has open cupping sessions.

Sip a Mayflower Tripel at the vintage brewery **Stadsbrouwerij De Pelgrim** (pictured above; p82) at Delfshaven, next to the Oude of Pelgrimvaderskerk, from where the Pilgrims set sail.

Enjoy Rotterdam craft brews beneath the crane of ex-shipyard **Oase** (p83).

FROM LEFT: BERTKNOT/FLICKR/CC BY-SA 2.0 DEED ©, EDWIN MULLER PHOTOGRAPHY/SHUTTERSTOCK ©

THE BEST

Art Experiences

In a region rich with artistic legacies – Vermeer spent his life in Delft and Rembrandt hailed from Leiden – the breadth of art here spans the works of Dutch Masters as well as boundary-pushing contemporary creators.

Be enthralled at Den Haag's **Mauritshuis**, displaying masterpieces such as Vermeer's *Girl With a Pearl Earring*; tickets also provide access to the Galerij Prins Willem V (p114).

Step inside the world's first open-access museum storage facility, **Depot Boijmans Van Beuningen**, hosting the collection of under-renovation Museum Boijmans Van Beuningen (p38).

Explore Rotterdam's contemporary arts scene at **Kunstinstituut Melly**, part of the Kunstblock (Art Block) on Witte de Withstraat (p51).

Trace Rembrandt's beginnings in Leiden, from where he studied to his early works, at the **Museum De Lakenhal** (p136).

Take in the huge 19th-century panorama of Scheveningen, **Panorama Mesdag**, from the upper platfom (p121).

View the world's largest collection of Piet Mondrian's paintings at the **Kunstmuseum Den Haag** (p124).

Right: Mauritshuis (p114)

THE BEST

Outdoor Experiences

In fine weather, Rotterdam and its surrounds have fantastic opportunities to get active, from cycling in urban areas and classic Dutch countryside to surfing and paddling by SUP along the waterways.

Ride the waves while surrounded by skyscrapers at **RiF010 Urban Surf Rotterdam** (pictured above; p44), a 2024-realised dream to bring surfing to the city centre.

Hop on a bike in Leiden to cycle through bulb fields in the **Bollenstreek** (p136), blooming with tulips in spring.

Escape Rotterdam's concrete, glass and steel jungle in expansive **Kralingse Bos** (p61), with walking and cycling paths, horse riding, and water sports on its lake.

Head to Scheveningen's sandy beach to take to the waves with surf schools and rentals, or get above them with Vissershavenweg's **Kitesurf School** (p124).

Abseil from the top of Rotterdam's iconic 1960 observation tower, the **Euromast**. (pictured above; p78).

Paddle through Delft's exquisite canalscapes on a SUP (stand-up paddleboard) with **Sup & Surf Delft** (p106).

EQROY/SHUTTERSTOCK ©

Maritiem Museum Rotterdam (p49)

THE BEST

Nautical Experiences

Europe's largest port, Rotterdam is the ultimate place to fathom the seafaring Netherlands, with unique opportunities to take to the water here as well as in the surrounding regions, including some places reached by boat.

Cruise with **Koninklijke Spido** (p49) to see Rotterdam's harbour and changing skyline, or take a longer excursion out to its huge container port.

Embark on the Holland-America Line's grand steam liner, the **SS Rotterdam** (p90), now permanently moored, with tours above and below deck.

Engage in interactive exhibits, watch blacksmiths at work and climb onto historic ships in the harbour outside the **Maritiem Museum Rotterdam** (p49).

Catch the Waterbus to **Kinderdijk** (p132), a beautiful UNESCO World Heritage site of waterways lined by 19 towering traditional windmills.

Rent an electric boat from **Bootjes en Broodjes** (p139) to navigate the web of picturesque canals threaded through the historic university city of Leiden.

Hortus Botanicus Leiden (p137)

THE BEST

Museum Experiences

Learn the stories of Rotterdam, its surrounds and its people by visiting some excellent museums that will leave you with a deeper understanding of how these places came to be as they are today.

Uncover the impact of WWII's bombings and view moving personal items at the **Museum Rotterdam '40-'45 NU** (p74).

See history through the photographer's lens at the **Nederlands Fotomuseum** (p90) in its striking new home, the Pakhuis Santos on the Rijnhaven.

Brace yourself for ghoulish torture instruments on display at the medieval prison **Rijksmuseum de Gevangenpoort** (p122), part of Den Haag's original fortifications.

Celebrate global cultures at the city's ethnographic world museum, the **Wereldmuseum Rotterdam** (p48).

Visit Leiden's 'living museum' botanic gardens, **Hortus Botanicus Leiden** (pictured above; p137), with its historic observatory.

Delve into the human story of migration at 2025-opening **FENIX** (p91).

Best for Kids

Join creatures such as adorable penguins for lunch (check for animal feeding times) at Rotterdam's conservation-led zoo, **Diergaarde Blijdorp** (p64).

Clamber aboard historic ships docked outside the fantastic **Maritiem Museum Rotterdam** (p49) and get hands-on learning about shipping operations inside, using crane simulators and steering ships.

Feel like a giant as you walk around Den Haag's wonderful amusement park **Madurodam** (p126); the Netherlands in miniature, it's home to tiny versions of Dutch landmarks you've seen on your trip.

Gaze bravely down below your feet through the Euroscoop lift's glass floor as it glides to the top of the **Euromast** (p78), looking out over the city.

Learn about natural history, from fossils to Rotterdam's surprising biodiversity, at **Het Natuurhistorisch Museum** (p47); on Wednesday admission for kids is free.

Best for Free

See the magical skyline views of Rotterdam from the roof garden of **Depot Boijmans Van Beuningen** (p38) for free on nights when its restaurant (and direct-access lift) is open.

Enter the exquisite 19th-century garden **Historische Tuin Schoonoord** (p79), a former country estate hidden next to Het Park, for free.

Take a free audio tour of the visitor centre at Den Haag's Peace Palace, the **Vredespaleis** (p125), home to the UN's Permanent Court of Arbitration and International Court of Justice.

Catch urban architecture, design and digital culture exhibitions at Museumpark design hub **Het Nieuwe Instituut** (p45) for free on Thursday evenings.

Head to cutting-edge Witte de Withstraat gallery **Kunstinstituut Melly** (p51) on Friday evenings for Kunstavond events, when admission to exhibitions and programs is free.

Perfect Days

Start by exploring Rotterdam; these itineraries will give you a taste of the city's highlights. With more time, venture into the wider region, visiting Kinderdijk, Den Haag, Delft and Leiden.

DAY ONE

Only Have One Day?

MORNING

Begin at the **Depot Boijmans Van Beuningen** (pictured above; p38) for an eye-opening look behind the scenes of the under-renovation Museum Boijmans Van Beuningen's collection. The Depot's bowl-shaped mirrored building is a work of art in itself. Don't miss the skyline views from the roof.

AFTERNOON

After checking out other Museumpark sights such as **Huis Sonneveld** (p36), head east along bar-and-gallery-lined Witte de Withstraat to the Leuvehaven to explore all things nautical, including ships moored out front, at the **Maritiem Museum Rotterdam** (p49).

EVENING

Take a watertaxi to **Hotel New York** (p92) for dinner and drinks on its terrace looking back at the city skyline.

Erasmusbrug (p89)

DAY TWO

A Weekend Trip

MORNING

Parqiet (p75) is a lovely spot for breakfast in the greenery of **Het Park** (p78). Head up the adjacent **Euromast** (p78) tower (daredevils could even abseil down).

AFTERNOON

Walk west to the picturesque port of Delfshaven, one of Rotterdam's few neighbourhoods to escape wartime destruction. Have a beer at the **Stadsbrouwerij De Pelgrim** (p82), and stop in at the **Dutch Pinball Museum** (p79) to play its vintage machines.

EVENING

Make your way to the **Hofbogen** (pictured above; p64) former railway viaduct in Noord to browse its archway shops and stop for dinner at its restaurants and eateries, such as the food hall inside the former **Station Bergweg** (p66).

DAY THREE

A Short Break

MORNING

Rotterdam's **Markthal** (pictured above; p44) is a striking place to start: admire its architecture and ceiling mural, and browse its food and drink stands. Continue to **RiF010 Urban Surf Rotterdam** (p44) to catch some waves in its open-air pool in the centre of the city, or watch the action from its **Surfbar & Kitchen** (p53) terrace.

AFTERNOON

From the graceful span of the **Erasmusbrug** (p89), sail by Waterbus to UNESCO World Heritage–listed **Kinderdijk** (p132) to stroll or cycle along its peaceful towpaths lined by traditional windmills.

EVENING

Return by Waterbus to Rotterdam. Dine on seafood at **Zeezout** (p53). Finish the night listening to live jazz at **Dizzy** (p82).

More time? Discover Den Haag

MORNING

Den Haag, seat of government and royalty, deserves a day of exploration. Start at its **Grote Kerk** (p122); its tower can be climbed. Walk along the Gravenstraat to the **Hofvijver** (p123) lake across from the centuries-old **Binnenhof** (p123) (currently undergoing a massive, multiyear renovation). Head to the wonderful **Mauritshuis** (p114) to see masterpieces such as Vermeer's incomparable *Girl with a Pearl Earring*. If you're a fan of MC Escher's mind-bending designs, you'll want to visit **Escher in Het Paleis** (p116).

AFTERNOON

Take a stroll through a delightful miniature Netherlands at amusement park **Madurodam** (pictured below; p126), at the edge of forest Scheveningen Bosjes. The west-facing strand at **Scheveningen** (p123) is a wonderful place to watch the sunset, with plenty of beachside bars.

EVENING

Back in Den Haag's city centre, catch a music or dance performance at splendid multi-venue cultural centre **Amare** (p125), and finish the night with heist-themed cocktails at the **Gold Bar** (p129), housed in the Netherlands' former gold reserve bank vault.

Madurodam (p126)

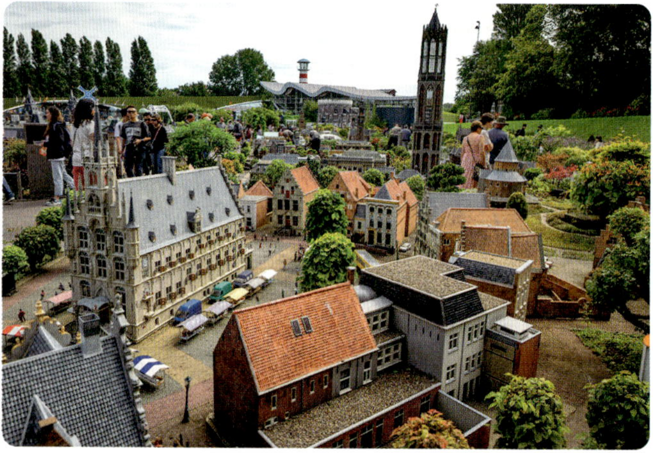

A Delft Day Trip

Vermeer's hometown, Delft, is a treasure. The town is synonymous with its blue-painted delftware porcelain, still hand-crafted at **Royal Delft** (pictured above; p105). Take a tour of the factory and stay for lunch at its cafe.

Hop on a **Rondvaartdelft** (p106) boat tour around Delft's canals; if it's warm, you could also explore them by paddleboard with **Sup & Surf Delft** (p106). Afterwards, climb the 376 steps to the top of the **Nieuwe Kerk** (p104), and reward yourself with a beer on the **Markt** (p104).

Dine at 16th-century storehouse **De Centrale** (p107) and finish the night at one of the bars surrounding the **Beestenmarkt**.

Side Trip to Leiden

Stroll along Leiden's canals to see Rembrandt's early work at the **Museum De Lakenhal** (p136) and retrace the Dutch Master's early steps, visiting the **Young Rembrandt Studio** (p138).

Head to the **Hortus Botanicus** (p137) to discover rare plants collected from around the world, and the world's oldest university **observatory** (p137). Leiden's many learned museums include the National Museum of Antiquities, the **Rijksmuseum van Oudheden** (pictured above; p136). If it's tulip season you could catch the glorious displays at **Keukenhof** (p138).

Have dinner at **Lot en de Walvis** (p137) at the old harbour, before walking back along the Herengracht for drinks at the bars surrounding the Koornbrug.

Get Prepared

BOOK AHEAD

Three months before
Be sure to book your accommodation with plenty of time to spare – hotels here fill up fast.

One month before
Increasingly, museum entry requires you to reserve a time slot online. Popular places can fill up in advance, so book ahead.

One week before
Check the Agenda section of the Rotterdam Tourist Information website to find out what festivals and events are on, and reserve tickets.

Manners Matter

Rotterdammers are relaxed and down-to-earth, and pretty well anything goes, but respecting others is paramount (queue jumping is frowned upon). Punctuality is highly regarded; tardiness is considered impolite.

The Dutch are renowned straight talkers. Don't be offended if locals give you their frank, unvarnished opinion. It's not considered impolite; rather, it comes from the desire to be honest and communicate clearly.

The Netherlands Defined

Though you might hear references to 'Holland', of the Netherlands' 12 provinces, Holland comprises just two: Noord-Holland (North Holland; home to the national capital Amsterdam) and Zuid-Holland (South Holland; where Rotterdam, Delft, Den Haag, Kinderdijk, Gouda, Leiden and the Bollenstreek are all located); the populous conurbation spanning both provinces plus Utrecht is the Randstad. The country as a whole is the Netherlands, not Holland, even if tourism branding isn't always clear.

Things to Know

Accommodation When booking accommodation, know what to expect. Older buildings might not have air conditioning or lifts (and staircases are narrow and steep). Liberal attitudes mean bathrooms may be open-plan and/or have limited screening (sometimes even the toilets).

Weekly closures The majority of museums, and quite often shops and restaurants, close on Monday. Start a long weekend on a Friday instead.

Safety In Rotterdam, areas to exercise caution, especially at night, are around Centraal and Blaak train stations, between Delfshaven and Schiedam in West, and farther-flung parts of Zuid. Monitor government alerts on your country's travel advisory or at english.nctv.nl.

Language Fluent English is widely spoken, but using a few words of Dutch is appreciated and will enrich your trip.

TIPPING

The Dutch do tip, but modestly and not always.

Restaurants & cocktail bars
Or round up

Other bars, pubs & cafes

Taxis

Hotel porters

DAILY BUDGET

Budget: Less than €150

- Dorm bed: €35–60
- Frites: €4
- Burger and beer: €20
- Laurenskerk tower climb: €7.50
- Watertaxi ride: €5

Midrange: €150–300

- Double room: from €120
- Sandwich: €8–12
- Two-course dinner and cocktail: €35–55
- Depot Boijmans Van Beuningen ticket: €20
- Koninklijke Spido 75-minute harbour tour: €17.50

Top end: More than €300

- Luxurious hotel double room: from €200
- Restaurant main course at lunch: €20–30
- Top restaurant seven-course menu with wine pairings: €120
- Concert at De Doelen: €30–80
- Private boat rental per day: from €260

Currency
Euro (€)

Language
Dutch (English widely spoken)

Time
Central European Time (GMT/UTC plus one hour)

NISSRINE MAHMOUD/SHUTTERSTOCK ©

TIP

Download the handy Rotterdam Tourist App, with maps, event listings, travel planners and much more, and sign up for a free Rotterdam City Card (rotterdam.info) for discounts on some sights.

When To Go

Any time of year Rotterdam has perennial and ephemeral attractions that vary by season, giving you plenty of reasons to visit (and revisit).

Seasons will have a big impact on your visit to Rotterdam and the surrounding region. Summer sees warm temperatures, park picnics, beach trips, boating and water sports, and festivals galore. The cultural season kicks off in autumn; by winter, which can be rainy, snowy and windy (especially by the water), the action shifts indoors, when the Dutch quality of *gezelligheid* (conviviality, cosiness) is at its best in the city's cafes and creative spaces. Spring sees the countryside burst into colour, with tulips blooming in the nearby Bollenstreek's bulb fields.

The Big Events

January/February: Kicking the year off, the **International Film Festival Rotterdam (IFFR)** is an annual film festival held over 11 days in locations around Rotterdam, including **Schouwburgplein** (p52). Independent and experimental films are the focus, with the Tiger Awards recognising up-and-coming international film talent.

June: Over 125 activities (tours, workshops, exhibitions, films...) across 40 locations celebrate the city's biggest claim to fame during **De Rotterdam Architectuur Maand (Rotterdam Architecture Month)**.

July: For three days in mid-July the world's largest indoor music festival, the **North Sea Jazz Festival**, features more than a thousand musicians in 150 performances across 15 stages at arena complex Rotterdam Ahoy. Hofbogen jazz club **Bird** (p64) hosts the afterparty.

September: Rotterdam's port is in the spotlight for three days in early

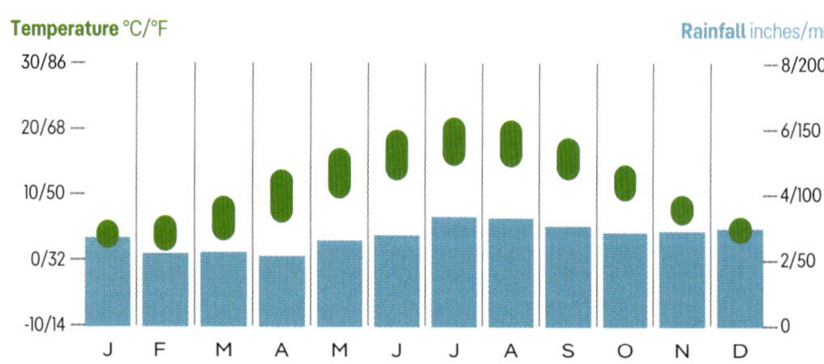

BEN HOUDIJK/SHUTTERSTOCK ©

North Sea Jazz Festival

September during the **World Port Days**. Crowds flock to the waterfront for boat parades, Royal Navy displays, huge ships, flyovers, music and spectacular firework displays.

Artsy & Interesting

April: An 1824 church, the Havenkerk is the location of the three-day **Nederlands Jeneverfestival Schiedam**, with an array of events including *jenever* (traditional Dutch gin) masterclasses and cocktail competitions.

May: The **Rotterdamse Dakendagen (Rotterdam Rooftop Days)** highlight Rotterdam's 'roofscape' for a week in May, with special-access visits, concerts and talks that reveal a whole new side of the city.

June: For three days in late June the **Noordplein** (p63) fills with music and stalls during the **Rotterdam Bluegrass Festival**.

August: Screened in a sculpture garden under the stars, **Roffa Mon Amour** is an opportunity to check out diverse films as well as Keilewerf art centre Brutus (a self-described cross between a 'maze and time machine, bomb shelter and launch pad, laboratory and industrial ruin, curiosities cabinet and think tank').

ACCOMMODATION

Rotterdam gets busiest between May and September, when the weather is at its warmest, and also draws crowds during special events. The shoulder-season months of April (King's Day celebrations aside) and October are good for finding more accommodation availability at cheaper prices. Always book ahead.

Getting There

Most visitors arrive at Amsterdam's Schiphol airport or by rail at Rotterdam's international train station, Centraal. Rotterdam also has its own smaller airport, and ferries serving Hoek van Holland.

Points of Entry

Rotterdam Centraal Station

Rotterdam's state-of-the-art Centraal Station is located in Rotterdam Centrum, on the edge of Noord. Eurostar has services to London (3¼ hours), Brussels (70 minutes) and Paris (2¾ hours). European Sleeper runs overnight three times weekly to Berlin and on to Prague. International bus operator FlixBus (*flixbus.nl*) stops on Conradstraat, outside Centraal's western exit. Direct services include Amsterdam, Berlin, Brussels, Copenhagen and Paris.

Rotterdam The Hague Airport

Rotterdam The Hague Airport, serving 50 European destinations, is less than 6km north-west of Rotterdam. Bus 33 links the airport with Meijersplein, from where you can take metro line E south to Rotterdam or north to Den Haag. A taxi from the airport to Rotterdam's city centre costs around €37.50 and takes about 15 minutes.

Hoek van Holland

Stena Line has overnight services from Harwich, England, to Hoek van Holland, 28km north-west of Rotterdam's city centre. Metro line B connects it with West Blaak station in Centrum.

From Schiphol Airport

By Train

Amsterdam's Schiphol airport is 58km north of Rotterdam. Its train station is under the arrivals hall. Direct Sprinter trains run to Rotterdam (from €14.50, 50 minutes), stopping at destinations including Leiden, Den Haag and Delft en route. Faster InterCity Direct trains (extra €2.90 supplement, 30 minutes) make no stops. No buses run between Schiphol and Rotterdam.

ETIAS

In 2025, European Travel Information and Authorisation System (ETIAS) preauthorisation will be needed for visitors from over 60 visa-exempt countries. It costs €7; apply online at travel-europe .europa.eu/etias.

Getting Around

Rotterdam is walkable and flat, although outside the city centre its neighbourhoods are quite spread out. As elsewhere in the Netherlands, cycling is a popular mode of transport, and the city also has an integrated system of metros, trams, buses and zippy harbour watertaxis. Delft and Den Haag are connected to Rotterdam by train.

Bicycle

Bike rentals are easy to come by around the city. Outlets include **Zwaan Bikes**, just west of Rotterdam Centraal Station, which has city/electric bikes (per day from €15/27.50) and **Centrum Bikes** (city/electric bikes per day from €17.50/30), just south of Beurs metro station, next to the Leuvehaven. Alternatively, find share bikes through the apps Donkey Republic (*donkey.bike*) or Listnride (*listnride.com*).

For short distances and day trips, the *fietsknooppuntennetwerk* (cycle junction network), made up of *knooppunten* (junctions, ie 'nodes') where cycle routes converge, is easily navigable. Route-finding apps include the Fietsersbond Routeplanner (*routeplanner.fietsersbond.nl*).

For long-distance cycling journeys, check out the Landelijke Fietsroutes (LF routes), which continue to expand and are downloadable on a handy app (*nederlandfietsland.nl/fietsapps*).

Helmets aren't mandatory in the Netherlands but can be a literal life-saver; you can hire them from bike-rental outlets.

FROM LEFT: VECTOR-HUB/SHUTTERSTOCK ©, ALEXANDROS MICHAILIDIS/SHUTTERSTOCK ©

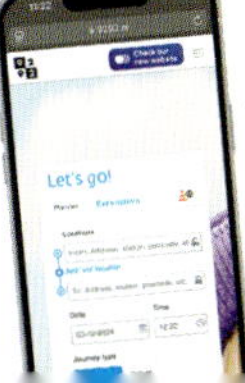

ESSENTIAL APP

Journey planner 9292.nl calculates the most efficient route in real time and estimates costs.

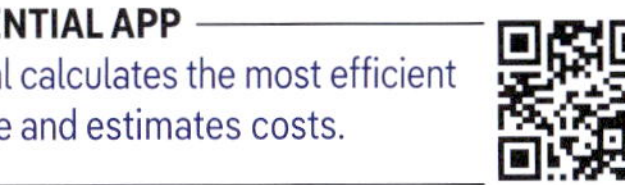

Metro

Quick and efficient, Rotterdam's metro is the fastest way to cover long distances. Its five metro lines run north, south, east and west of the centre.

Tram

Trams cover most areas of Rotterdam, except along the waterfront.

Bus

Buses cover mostly residential areas that are not served by tram; visitors are unlikely to use them.

Watertaxi

Fast black-and-yellow watertaxis (*watertaxirotterdam.nl*) stop at 50 small piers on the Nieue Maas. It's an exhilarating way to travel and see the city from the water.

Fares are zoned; trips in central Rotterdam cost €5; across two zones €8; and across all three zones, from Oud-IJsselmonde in the east to Schiedam Vijfsluizen in the west, €12.50. Children under 12 pay half-price.

Waterbus

From its dock at Rotterdam's Erasmusbrug in Centrum, **Waterbus** (*waterbus.nl*) line 21 sails to the UNESCO-listed windmills at Kinderdijk, Molenkade, and line 20 to the charming town of Dordrecht, Merwekade. Pay by OV-chipkaart or buy e-tickets online; a day ticket (adult/child €15.50/5) allows unlimited travel.

Public Transport Essentials

- Rotterdam's public transport is operated by RET (*ret.nl*).
- The public transport ticketing system covers the entire country.
- For single trips you can buy a disposable OV-chipkaart (which incurs a €1 surcharge per journey on top of the standard fare). A single-trip ticket, valid for two hours, costs €4.50.
- For multiple journeys you can buy a reusable OV-chipkaart or use OVpay (a digital OV-pas is being rolled out, but the OV-chipkaart system will remain in use until at least the end of 2025).
- Fares are based on distance travelled; there are no zones.
- Hold an OV-chipkaart or OVpay against the reader to 'check in' when entering transport and 'check out' when exiting (or forfeit your deposit).
- A reusable OV-chipkaart costs €7.50 and is valid for five years. You then load it with credit at ticket machines. There's a minimum €10/20/4 for buses/trains/other forms of transport (eg trams); it's held as a deposit during your journey and the balance is refunded afterwards.

These reusable cards are automatically activated if bought from train stations; otherwise, you may need to activate it for 'pre-paid travel without NS subscription' at station ticket machines or service desks.

- An alternative to a physical OV-chipkaart is OVpay, using a contactless debit/credit card (Maestro, V PAY, Mastercard or Visa only) to 'check in' and 'check out' of your journey. It saves the cost of the reusable card or disposable card surcharge, though you're only able to track the fare in your card/bank statement (tallied and charged once per day).
- A good-value option if you're travelling further afield is to pick up a Tourist Day Ticket (€15.50), covering all of Zuid-Holland, including Lisse, Leiden, Den Haag, Delft, Kinderdijk, Gouda, Dordrecht and Rotterdam itself.

RET INFORMATION

The **RET information booth** sells tickets and is located in Centraal Station's main entrance hall.

Rotterdam to Delft

From Rotterdam Centraal Station (pictured right), take Sprinter or Intercity trains to Delft (tickets from €3.90; from 12 minutes).

Rotterdam to Den Haag

From Rotterdam Centraal, catch metro line E (from €5.30; 27 minutes) to Den Haag Centraal; alternatively, Sprinter and Intercity trains run via Delft to Den Haag Centraal (from €5.70, 30 minutes).

ANKOR LIGHT/SHUTTERSTOCK ©

A Few Surprises

In a city packed with surprises (the only shock would be anything run-of-the-mill), you'll find unique perspectives and one-of-a-kind experiences.

Floating Structures

Undaunted by the fact that 85% of the city lies up to 7m below sea level, Rotterdam is coming up with inspired concepts for floating structures that include the under-construction Rijnhaven development's floating parks; the world's largest sustainable office, FOR (Floating Offices Rotterdam), with a bar-restaurant, Putaine; and even dairy cows on a **Floating Farm** (p80) with its own shop.

Viewpoints

In a country as flat as the Netherlands, viewpoints let you look out over the lay of the land. As well as skyscrapers and church towers that you can climb to take in the views, quirkier options include the Hofbogen's Luchtpark (Air Park) and Luchtsingel (Air Canal), observation platforms like the 1960-built Euromast, and the spiralling 'tornado' atop the 2025-opening migration museum **FENIX** (p91).

Miniature Worlds

Putting the city and country under a microscope provides a new perspective. Indoor **Miniworld Rotterdam** (p78) has an astonishingly detailed recreation of the city, with model railways, a working port and simulated day and night. In Den Haag, outdoor **Madurodam** (p126) lets you walk around mini, operational scale versions of icons like Schiphol airport

Pinball

Pinball machines appear in all sorts of places, both expected (Scheveningen's pleasure pier) and unexpected (century-old railway station-turned-food hall, Station Bergweg). Rotterdam is even home to the **Dutch Pinball Museum** (p79), with over 100 playable vintage machines.

OFFBEAT ROTTERDAM

Catch some waves in a canal-turned-wave pool at **RiF010 Urban Surf Rotterdam** (p44), or rent SUPs to paddle through the city. Sail past huge ships carrying 20,000 containers, wind turbines being built and crane ships docking on a **Koninklijke Spido** (p49) port cruise. Ride a prewar tram through streets lined with 21st-century skyscrapers aboard **Lijn 10** (p48). Check out work by local artists in Delft's tiny telephone-box micro gallery **Voor de Kunst** (p103).

Miniworld Rotterdam (p78)

Dutch Pinball Museum (p79)

Explore Rotterdam

Rotterdam's Walking Tours

Delfshaven (p76)
ALEKSANDAR GEORGIEV/GETTY IMAGES ©

See p53
for eating,
drinking and
shopping
listings

Explore Centrum

Lively Centrum is Rotterdam's heart. Like its surrounds, the city's centre was flattened in WWII, rising phoenix-like over the decades since. Many of its landmark buildings date from the mid-20th century, with striking new structures continuing to redefine the skyline. Centrum, stretching from Centraal Station to the waterfront, contains the city's biggest-hitting cultural sights, especially south around Museumpark. It also has its greatest concentration of shops, restaurants and bars in the Cool District (especially on nightlife hub Witte de Withstraat), which unfolds to the east, taking in the fashionable streets around Meent and the spectacular Markthal, alongside Rotterdam's urban surf beach in the Steiger canal.

Getting Around

Train

Rotterdam Centraal Station is the gateway to this neighbourhood. You can transfer from intercity trains to metro and trams at both Centraal and Blaak Stations.

Metro

As well as metro stations at Rotterdam Centraal and Blaak, other handy metro stops include Beurs, Leuvehaven, Eendrachtsplein (for Museumpark) and Stadhuis.

Tram

Major stops include Centraal Station, Blaak, Stadhuis and Museumpark.

Ferry

Watertaxi docks include Boompjes, Leuvehaven/Mainport Hotel and Willemskade/Waterbus.

Timmerhuis (p41)

THE BEST

MUSEUM COLLECTION
Depot Boijmans Van Beuningen (p38)

SURFING
RIF010 Urban Surf Rotterdam (p44)

FOOD HALL
Markthal (p44)

SUSTAINABLE SHOPPING
De Groene Passage (p56)

HARBOUR TOUR
Koninklijke Spido (p49)

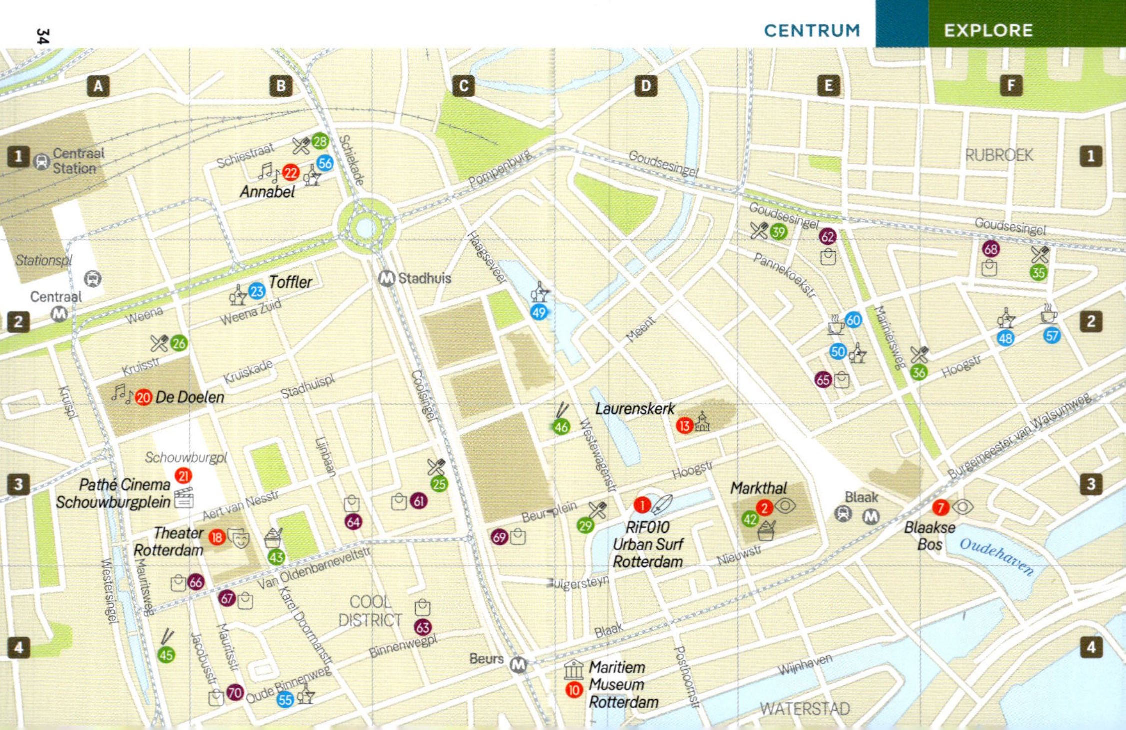
Centraal Station
Stationspl
Centraal
Weena
Kruisstr
Kruispl
De Doelen
Schiestraat
Annabel
Schiekade
Toffler
Weena Zuid
Kruiskade
Stadhuispl
Stadhuis
Pompenburg
Haagseveer
Coolsingel
Lijnbaan
Schouwburgpl
Pathé Cinema Schouwburgplein
Aert van Nesstr
Theater Rotterdam
Van Oldenbarneveltstr
Westersingel
Mauritsweg
Jacobusstr
Mauritsstr
Karel Doormanstr
Oude Binnenweg
COOL DISTRICT
Binnenwegpl
Beurs
Beursplein
Westewagenstr
Laurenskerk
Meent
Goudsesingel
Pannekoekstr
Marinierswg
Hoogstr
RiF010 Urban Surf Rotterdam
Bulgersteyn
Blaak
Maritiem Museum Rotterdam
Posthoornstr
Markthal
Nieuwstr
Blaak
Burgemeester van Walsumweg
Blaakse Bos
Oudehaven
Wijnhaven
WATERSTAD
RUBROEK

Nieuwe Binnenweg
Eendrachtsplein
Westblaak
Huis Sonneveld
WORM
MaMA
TR8 William Boothlaan
V2_
Witte de Withstr
Hartmansstr
Schilderstr
Het Nieuwe Instituut
Chabot Museum
Kunstinstituut Melly
DIJKZIGT
Museumpark
Museum Boijmans Van Beuningen
Depot Boijmans Van Beuningen
Schiedamse Vest
Schiedamsedijk
Leuvehaven
Scheepmakershaven
Boompjes
Nieuwe Maas
Maaskade
Eendrachtsweg
Vasteland
NOORDER EILAND
Prins Hendrikkade
Het Natuurhistorisch Museum
Kunsthal
Erasmus MC
Van Vollenhovenstr
Remastered
Lijn 10
Koninklijke Spido
Erasmusbrug
Westzeedijk
Willemskade
Kievitslaan
NIEUWE WERK
Parklaan
Veerhaven
Wereldmuseum Rotterdam
For more see
Top Experiences p36
Experiences p44
Eating p53
Drinking p55
Shopping p56
500 m
0.25 miles

★ TOP EXPERIENCE

Huis Sonneveld

Wing your way back to 1930s Rotterdam, when local architects were embracing Functionalism and designing streamlined and resolutely modern buildings for their clients to live and work in. The aesthetically pared-back but technology-rich Sonneveld House is one of the greatest examples of this significant architectural movement.

MAP P35 **A5**

PLANNING TIP
Book online, at Huis Sonneveld's entrance or at neighbouring architecture and design hub **Het Nieuwe Instituut**. There are combination tickets with Het Nieuwe Instituut, and with the Chabot Museum.

Scan this QR code for opening hours and other information.

The Architecture

When wealthy businessman Albertus Sonneveld decided to commission an architect to design a contemporary home for his family, the natural choice was Leendert van der Vlugt, who had designed the magnificent **Van Nelle Factory** (p72) where Sonneveld was a company director. Working with Johannes Brinkman, Van der Vlugt created a building that was hailed as an outstanding example of Dutch Functionalism as soon as it was completed in 1933. The house was restored in 2001 to reflect its condition when the Sonnevelds lived here, including many original furnishings, lighting and even utensils. It's now a national monument *(Huis Sonneveld only adult/child €10/free, combination ticket with Nieuwe Instituut €16.50/free).*

Distinctive Features

As you enter it's clear the house must have been unusual when it was built. Its colour scheme would have been considered daringly modern - especially the turquoise-blue tiles in the bathrooms.

Modern technologies are well represented, and the floors are covered in linoleum, a new and expensive product at the time. A separate 'Healthy House' audio tour explains how Huis Sonneveld was designed to be hygienic, minimising dust and bacteria and maximising clean air and sunlight.

FRED ROMERO FROM PARIS, FRANCE/WIKIMEDIA/CC BY 2.0

Staircases and narrow corridors mean the house isn't accessible for visitors with limited mobility, but it's possible to take a virtual-reality tour in the studio. New multisensory elements, such as 1930s music, touchable art and bathroom soap scents, open the house up to blind and partially sighted visitors.

The Sonnevelds

Multilanguage audio tours detail the history of the building and its occupants, and the custom-designed furniture, state-of-the-art appliances and advanced building techniques. Walking through the house – which is full of light, courtesy of banks of windows and a number of balconies – it's easy to imagine what life must have been like for the Sonneveld family and their staff. Kids can discover fun details about the house on a dedicated audio tour, 'Lodging with Leonard'.

QUICK BREAK

On the ground floor of Het Nieuwe Instituut, the bright, airy Nieuwe Café has a fantastic terrace, a casual vibe and a menu of mainly plant-based Afro-Caribbean, Asian and Mediterranean dishes.

★ TOP EXPERIENCE

Depot Boijmans Van Beuningen

Resembling a giant disco ball, this semi-spherical mirrored building is the storage facility for the 154,000-strong collection of masterpieces from Rotterdam's top art museum, the adjacent **Museum Boijmans Van Beuningen** (closed for renovations until 2029). In a world-first, you can go behind the scenes.

MAP P35 **A6**

PLANNING TIP
The Depot is closed on Monday. Time-slot tickets are only available online; if you're visiting on Thursday, Friday or Saturday, you can book combination tickets including dinner at Renilde restaurant.

Scan this QR code for opening hours and other information.

The Building

An instant icon when it was opened by King Willem-Alexander in 2021, this extraordinary structure (*adult/child €20/free*) is a work of art itself. Designed by Winy Maas of Rotterdam architectural firm MVRDV, it's covered by 1664 glass panels reflecting the surrounding Museumpark and city skyline.

Inside the bowl-shaped building, 15,541 sq metres of floor space wrap around a soaring 40m-high atrium, with a freestanding, curvilinear balcony, a labyrinth-like maze with floating display cases, glass walls where you can see artworks being unloaded, and windows giving you an unprecedented view of its operations, including unpacking and restoration – reinforcing that this isn't a museum but a working facility.

Visiting the Depot

The entire collection (only 8% of which could be displayed at any one time in the museum) is stored according to its requirements, with separate, climate-controlled compartments for paintings, black-and-white and colour photography, metals, plastics and organic media.

Valued at over €8 billion, the collection includes masterpieces by artists including Jan van Eyck, Hieronymous Bosch, Rubens, Rembrandt, Monet, Degas, Van Gogh, Picasso, Miró and Bacon. Artworks often move or are lent out, so you won't know what you might see leaning at unexpected angles against barriers and grates.

BERK OZDEMIR/SHUTTERSTOCK ©

Wandering through the transparent building with the free downloadable app is eye-opening, but it's especially worth booking in for a small-group guided tour (included in admission, but tours fill quickly) at the entrance hall's consoles when you arrive. Three 30-minute tours run per hour and take you into one of the storage compartments.

If there's an artwork you're keen to see, contact the depot in advance to find out if it's available for 'art by request' private viewings (*extra €50 plus admission*).

QUICK BREAK

On the rooftop, Renilde is a stunning spot to drop in for an inexpensive lunch or drink during your visit to the Depot. Reserve ahead for dinner (Thursday to Saturday).

The Rooftop

Planted with birch and pine trees, the roof garden has panoramic city views. During the day you'll need an admission ticket to reach it and its restaurant, Renilde, but it's also accessible via the express lift for free from 6pm to 10pm on nights the restaurant is open.

Walk Centrum: Architecture

WWII's bombardments left Rotterdam's centre in ruins, but rather than recreate the historic port local authorities embraced a fresh canvas for contemporary, sustainable architecture that shapes the city today. On this walk you'll see buildings that remain from the prewar city and those built in the decades since, including the city's latest, most exciting innovations.

START	END	LENGTH
Rotterdam Centraal Station (metro Centraal Station)	Witte Huis (metro Blaak)	4km; 3 hours

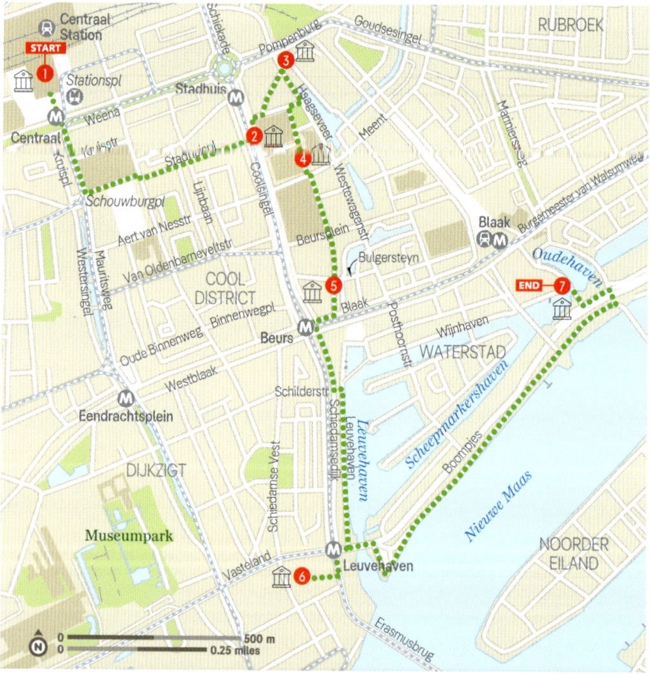

1 Grand Entrance

Rotterdam's **Centraal Station**, its dramatically angled passenger hall sporting a pointed, stainless-steel-clad roof, was designed by Benthem Crouwel, MVSA and West 8, and unveiled in 2013. On its western side you'll see the massive eight-storey, 120,000-sq-metre Groot Handelsgebouw (GHG; 1953), one of the first post-WWII buildings and a symbol of Rotterdam's reconstruction.

2 City Hall

Cross the Lijnbaan, Europe's first car-free street and the precursor to strip malls. On Coolsingel, Rotterdam's palatial Beaux Arts–style, sandstone-fronted **Stadhuis**, designed by HJ Evers, was built between 1914 and 1920 and survived WWII unscathed; its 71m clock tower is topped by a golden angel. (*Book free one-hour tours online.*)

3 Art Meets Architecture

Walk beneath Doelstraat's 1994 Günther Förg Tor arch before reaching the **Nieuwe Delftse Poort** (1995) by Cor Kraat, a skeletal 18m-wide, 13m-deep, 18m-high sculpture created to replace the 1764 city gate destroyed in WWII's bombardment, signifying that Rotterdam continues to build.

4 Sugar Cubes

The 1953 building where Rotterdam's reconstruction planning took place, the **Timmerhuis** was extended in 2015 by Pritzker-winning Rotterdam architect Rem Koolhaas of OMA (Office for Metropolitan Architecture). It's locally dubbed the 'sugar cubes' for its stepped aluminium-and-glass facade reflecting the sky.

5 Dutch Classicism

Walk south on the Rodezand, passing the sunken Beurstraverse (Koopgoot) shopping arcade and reflective Rotterdam World Trade Centre, to the exquisite **Schielandshuis**, designed by Pieter Post and completed in 1665, now housing municipal offices.

6 The Netherlands' Tallest Building

South, on Gedempte Zalmhaven, near the Erasmusbrug, the 2022-completed **Zalmhaven** scrapes the sky at 215m, with commercial and residential spaces and a restaurant, Celest, on the 57th and 58th floors, with views as far as Den Haag.

7 Europe's First Skyscraper

Head north-east along the Nieuwe Maas to the red-pylon Willemsbrug and cross the Oudehaven. Dating from 1897–98, the 11-storey, 45m-high **Witte Huis** (White House) was designed by Willem Molenbroek in Art Nouveau style using load-bearing brick walls rather than a steel skeleton. De Rotterdam Tours' Markthal tours (p44) include a visit to the roof for views of the changing skyline.

WALKING TOUR

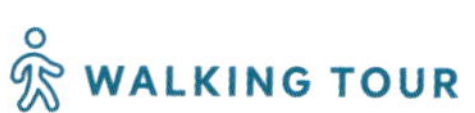

Walk Centrum: Public Art

In Rotterdam's art-filled centre, this walk gives you a sense of the city's many facets, including its high-rise-lined boulevards, canals, squares and bustling shopping streets, while also telling its story, past, present and future, through a multitude of thought-provoking and striking sculptures by artists both historic (including de Keyser, Rodin and Picasso) and contemporary.

START	END	LENGTH
Beeld van Erasmus (metro Blaak)	L'homme qui marche (metro Eendrachtsplein)	2.2km; 2 hours

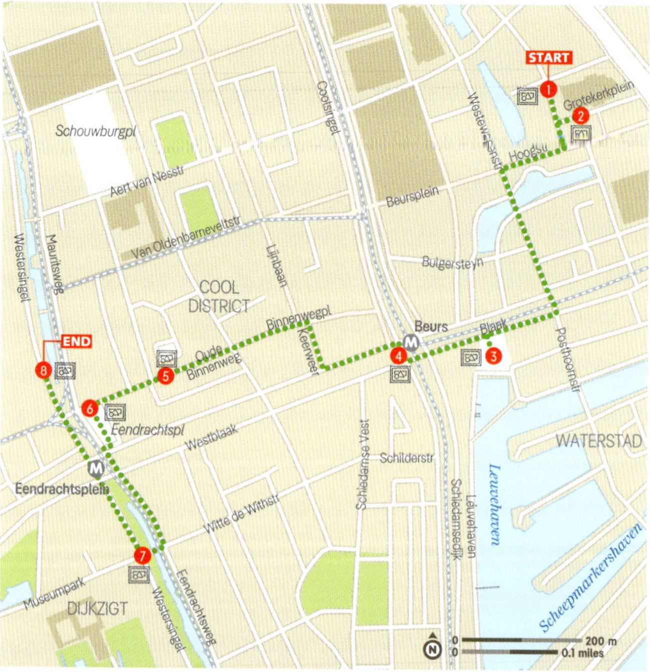

1 The Netherlands' Oldest Sculpture

Opposite the Laurenskerk on the Grotekerkplein, 1622 bronze sculpture **Beeld van Erasmus** by renowned architect and artist Hendrick de Keyser was unique in Europe at the time for honouring an intellectual figure: humanist, Catholic priest, theologian and philosopher Desiderius Erasmus Roterodamus (Erasmus of Rotterdam).

2 Erasmus' Birthplace

On the Laurenskerk's southern side, the 2016 Erasmus Monument, by Diana de Graaf, **Maaike Disco and Reinier de Gooijer**, marks the location where Erasmus was born on 28 October 1466. This freestanding recreated wall of his house is superimposed with Erasmus' portrait, made up of majolica tiles with quotes from his texts that become visible as you approach.

3 The Destroyed City

Head south-west to Rotterdam's urban surf canal Steigersgracht and cross Blaak to Leuvehaven. On a basalt pedestal, bronze sculpture **De Verwoeste Stad** (1953), by Ossip Zadkine, portrays an anguished human figure with hands raised skywards and a hole in his chest, symbolising Rotterdam's heart lost during WWII's destruction.

4 Stop Oil

At the intersection of Blaak and Coolsingel, Joep van Lieshout's 2010 sculpture **Cascade**, an 8.5m-high dark-green plastic sculpture, represents the depletion of the earth's resources and the human cost through the limp, formless figures oozing from 18 oil barrels.

5 Neighbourhood Dog

Further west on Oude Binnenweg is one of the city's most beloved artworks, **Fikkie** (1963) by Joeki Simak, an adorable cast-bronze dog, who receives a winter scarf and a summer water bowl. In 1999 sculptor Hans Citroen added a bronze turd nearby.

6 Santa Claus

Continuing west, American artist Paul McCarthy's controversial bronze statue of a gnome-like **Santa Claus** (2001) holds what may (or may not) be a pine tree.

7 Picasso's Muse

South on Westersingel is Picasso's sandblasted-concrete sculpture **Sylvette** (1970), depicting his model and muse Sylvette David.

8 The Man Who Walks

At Eendrachtsplein, Rodin's headless 1907 sculpture **L'homme qui marche** was installed here in 1988. From the southern side the figure appears to be striding north along the canal, where another five sculptures make up the Westersingel Sculpture Route.

EXPERIENCES

Ride the Waves in Downtown Rotterdam

SURFING

MAP: 1 P34 D3

In an exhilarating world-first, you can surf year-round in the middle of the city at **RiF010 Urban Surf Rotterdam** (*rif010.nl; surf session/lesson from €45/50*). In the works for over a decade before launching in 2024, this open-air wave pool surrounded by skyscrapers has an energy-efficient design and a 100% sustainably generated wave pool with perfect broken and unbroken waves from 1m up to 1.6m (settings are adjusted for experience levels) every seven seconds.

For surfers who know the fundamentals, sessions start with a safety briefing before you get in on the beach side (De Baai), paddle to the Rif and wait in the takeoff-zone line – even at peak capacity you can catch upwards of 10 waves a session. Lessons are available for all levels of experience. Boards are provided, and wetsuits and other rentals are available. Bring swimwear and sunscreen and arrive around 45 minutes beforehand. Kids must be aged eight and over and able to swim. The facility's **RiF010 Surfbar & Kitchen** (p53) has a terrace overlooking the waves.

Taste Your Way Around Rotterdam's Markthal

MARKET, ARCHITECTURE

MAP: 2 P34 E3

Shaped like an enormous horseshoe, Rotterdam's landmark Markthal (*markthal.nl*) opened in 2014. Designed by MVRDV's Winy Maas (whose work includes the Depot Boijmans Van Beuningen (p38), the 40m-high, cathedral-inspired building incorporates 228 apartments within the arch. Inside, a giant 11,000-sq-metre mural, *Cornucopia* (Horn of Plenty), by artists Arno Coenen and Iris Roskam, with outsized, vividly coloured fruit and vegetables, flowers and insects recalling 17th-century Dutch still-life paintings, soars above 96 food stalls and 20 restaurants and food shops.

As well as fresh produce, meat and seafood, Dutch cheeses, nuts, spices, breads, pastries, juices, coffee, tea, craft beer, chocolate and confectionery, ready-to-eat snacks span local delicacies such as *stroopwafels* (caramel-syrup-filled wafers) and international bites (Spanish tapas, Greek street food, sushi...). There's a huge Albert Heijn supermarket below ground and Asian supermarket Wah Nam Hong on the 1st floor.

Behind-the-scenes one-hour visits with **De Rotterdam Tours** (*derotterdamweekendtours.nl; €17.95*) include a visit to the otherwise off-limits underground logistics centre, a glimpse of artefacts unearthed during construction, meeting a stallholder and tastings.

Catch Exhibitions & Events at the Kunsthal

GALLERY

MAP: 3 P34 B7

In a groundbreaking building designed in 1988–89 by world-renowned Rotterdam architect Rem Koolhaas together with Fuminori Hoshino of architectural firm OMA (Office for Metropolitan Architecture), and opened in 1992, the **Kunsthal** (*kunsthal.nl; adult/child €18/free*) is a key part of Museumpark's ensemble.

This 3300-sq-metre 'Art Hall' has no permanent collection – its seven exhibition spaces and 300-seat auditorium present a constantly changing and invariably thought-provoking programme of exhibitions.

In 2012 thieves stole seven paintings (two Monets and one each by Picasso, Gaugin, Matisse, Freud and de Haan) on loan from the Dutch Triton Foundation. The following year, it was discovered the paintings were likely destroyed in Romania by the mother of one of the thieves following his arrest, and in 2014 the Kunsthal underwent a major security upgrade and renovation (also by OMA).

There are always several exhibitions to visit – from painting to photography and from fashion to graphic design, and regular live events, talks and workshops. The gallery is closed on Monday (except holidays); prebooking online is advised.

Discover New Design Directions at Het Nieuwe Instituut

GALLERY

MAP: 4 P34 A5

Design-driven cultural hub **Het Nieuwe Instituut** (*nieuweinstituut.nl; adult/child including Huis Sonneveld €16.50/free*) holds the National Collection of Dutch Architecture and Urban Design, among the world's largest such

MUSEUMPARK

A greenery-filled 'city living room' with interconnected open-air spaces with shady trees, paths, terraces, water features and sculptures, Museumpark is flanked by cultural institutions. Anchored by the under-renovation Museum Boijmans Van Beuningen and its gleaming open-access storage facility Depot Boijmans Van Beuningen are design hub Het Nieuwe Instituut, containing the Dutch Architecture and Urban Planning National Collection; preserved 1933 villa Huis Sonneveld; the 1938 villa-housed International Expressionism Chabot Museum; dynamic gallery the Kunsthal; and kid-friendly Het Natuurhistorisch Museum, in the original estate's family home before the museum's – and park's – foundation in 1927.

collections, with some four million drawings, photographs, architectural models, and resources in its research centre (open Tuesday to Friday). Its exhibitions are fascinating for anyone interested in urban architecture, design and digital culture, as are regular events such as book launches and lectures (many in English).

Architect Jo Coenen beat high-profile competitors including Rem Koolhaas to win the 1988 design competition for the Museumpark building: a striking glass, concrete and steel structure incorporating multiple exhibition spaces, a 180-seat auditorium overlooking a lake, and a biodiverse garden.

While you can buy standalone tickets for neighbouring Huis Sonneveld (p36), it's not possible to buy tickets for Het Nieuwe Instituut alone, only combination tickets for the two. Het Nieuwe Instituut is closed on Monday; there's free admission on Thursday nights from 5pm.

There's a great design bookshop, too; its cafe is a popular meeting spot.

View Expressionist Art in the Chabot Museum's Modernist Villa

GALLERY

MAP: 5 P34 A5

A Museumpark gem, the **Chabot Museum** (*chabotmuseum.nl; adult/child €12/free*) is set in one of the city's most distinctive pre-WWII villas, now a national monument. Enveloped by greenery, the gleaming-white building with stark lines and curved balconies was designed in 1938 by GW (Gerrit Willem) Baas, who worked for Brinkman & Van der Vlugt – architects of Huis Sonneveld (p36) and UNESCO-listed Van Nelle Fabriek (p72) in West – as a private residence for the Kraaijeveld family. Since 1993 its light-filled interior has been home to the Chabot Museum, showcasing paintings and sculptures by leading Dutch expressionist Henk Chabot (1894–1949). Chabot's dramatic works, created at his home on the Rotte river, capture the emotions of farmers, gardeners and Rotterdammers as they hid and fled hardship during WWII. Regular temporary exhibitions also take place here.

The museum closes on Monday. There are combination tickets available with Huis Sonneveld (*adult/child €18/free*). If you're booking a museum-organised Saturday-afternoon guided tour of Van Nelle Fabriek, note it includes entry to the Chabot Museum.

Take a Natural History Lesson at Kid-friendly Het Natuurhistorisch

MUSEUM

MAP: 6 P34 A7

Occupying the 19th-century red-brick Villa Dijkzigt at Museumpark, built in 1852 by JF Metzelaar for the Van Hoboken family and extended in 1995 by Erick van Egeraat to incorporate a glass pavilion, Rotterdam's 1927-opened natural history museum **Het Natuurhistorisch** (*hetnatuurhistorisch.nl; adult/child €11/5.50*) is fun for all ages but especially for kids. It looks at the natural world in a fun and accessible way, such as re-envisaging Rotterdam as a national park now and in the future, with urban reserves, green corridors and 'stepping stones' to boost biodiversity in the city; checking out fossils found in the Netherlands; viewing displays from the museum's 400,000-strong collection of butterflies, beetles, molluscs, plants, fish and birds as well as marine mammals; and learning about local wildlife that has died as a result of litter, pollution and human activity and how to protect it and help it thrive. In addition to permanent exhibitions, there are regular temporary exhibitions.

Kids get free admission on Wednesday. The museum is closed on Monday.

Step Inside Rotterdam's Iconic Cube Houses ARCHITECTURE

Designed by Dutch architect Piet Blom and built between 1982 and 1984, the mind-bending **Blaakse Bos** (MAP: 7 P34 **F3**) is a 'forest' of 38 cube-shaped apartments perched on hexagonal pylons. This vibrant yellow-and-white-coloured, crazily tilting apartment complex is one of the city's most recognisable structures.

One apartment, the **Kijk-Kubus Museumwoning** (see 7 P34 **F3**; *kubuswoning.nl; adult/child €3/1.50*), is open daily to the public. Here, you'll get a feel for what it's like to live in one of Rotterdam's most famous structures, the 45-degree-slanted 'cube houses'. Climb the steep, narrow stairs to the show cube's 100-sq-metre interior over three levels – the kitchen and living room, bathroom and bedrooms, and loft – with furniture custom built to fit the odd angles.

Markthal tours with De Rotterdam Tours (p44) also include show-cube entry.

REBUILDING AFTER THE WWII BLITZ

Rotterdam changed forever on 14 May 1940, when 90 Luftwaffe planes dropped more than 1000 bombs on the city, levelling the medieval centre and many neighbourhoods. The Blitz killed more than 900 people, and destroyed at least 24,000 homes, 24 churches, 2000 shops, 775 warehouses and 62 schools. Some 80,000 Rotterdammers were made homeless. Reconstruction architect Cornelis van Traa devised a completely new spatial layout. New residential areas were built on the outskirts and the centre gained high-rise commercial buildings and innovations such as the Lijnbaan strip mall. The era of experimentation in urban design and architecture had arrived, and continues here today.

Rotterdam's **Stayokay** (see 7 P34 **F3**) youth hostel occupies the supersized cube at the southern end.

Nearby is another of Piet Blom's creations, the 61m-high Blaaktoren (1984) residential high-rise, better known – and instantly identifiable – as the Potlood (Pencil) for its tall, straight lines and pointy top.

Travel the Globe at the Wereldmuseum

MUSEUM

MAP: 8 P34 **C8**

Over 170 nationalities call Rotterdam home, and more than half of this port city's population have culturally diverse roots, which goes to the heart of the **Wereldmuseum Rotterdam** (*rotterdam.wereldmuseum.nl; adult/child €16/8*). Its spectacular setting is the mansion built in 1851 for the Royal Yacht Club on Willemskade, which became an ethnographic museum in 1885, when Dutch trade, colonialism and missionary work were prevalent. Its focus later shifted to anthropological aspects. Now, alongside the Wereldmuseum Amsterdam (formerly the Tropenmuseum) and Wereldmuseum Leiden, it celebrates global cultures.

The museum (closed Monday except holidays) centres on semipermanent exhibition Kruispunt Rotterdam (Crossroads Rotterdam), with artefacts, artistic treasures such as textiles, films, contemporary artworks and music, and eye-opening temporary exhibitions that might highlight how global colonialism's legacy is reflected in the city today or explore China's culture of making. On Wednesday, weekends and holidays, there's also an interactive children's exhibition, Superstreet (in Dutch, with some guidance in English), where kids encounter multinational neighbours. There's a waterside cafe and gift shop.

Ride a Vintage Tram Through Rotterdam

TRAM TOUR

MAP: 9 P34 **D7**

On weekends from May to October as well as Thursday and Friday from early June to mid-September, **Lijn 10** (*Line 10; rovm.nl; adult/child €15/8*) circumnavigates the city.

Starting from Willemsplein, these hop-on, hop-off historic tram tours, typically aboard 1931 four-axle tram cars, travel around Centrum and West as far as historic Delfshaven, with some tours crossing the Erasmusbrug (aka 'Swan' bridge). En route you'll pass some of Rotterdam's most iconic sights, with multilingual commentary. A full circuit takes around 75 minutes. Tickets are sold on board and are valid all day.

It's operated by the Rotterdam Openbaar Vervoer Museum (*Rotterdam Public Transport Museum; adult/child €7.50/5*), in a 1923 heritage tram depot north of the city at Hillegersberg, which opens on a handful of Saturdays during the year. There's transport to/from the museum by vintage tram – check the website for details.

Clamber Aboard Historic Ships at the Maritiem Museum Rotterdam

MUSEUM

MAP: 10 P34 D4

Overlooking Leuvehaven, the **Maritiem Museum Rotterdam** (*maritiemmuseum.nl; adult/child €17.50/12.50*), closed Monday, is a kid favourite, with exhibits such as model ships and displays showing how over the centuries Rotterdam came to be the largest port in Europe, and entertaining hands-on exhibits such as the 'Offshore Experience', which investigates day-to-day operations on North Sea oil and gas platforms; participants can text their dexterity with crane simulators, take safety quizzes, steer ships with a joystick and more.

In the Leuve Pavilion, you can learn about shipbuilding and maintenance, and often see blacksmith demonstrations and artisans such welders and carpenters at work.

For many the true stars are docked outside; tickets include entry to the museum's collection of historic vessels and cranes moored in the Leuvehaven; all are in working order and many can be boarded. Visiting ships (tall ships, fishing vessels, patrol boats) also stop by. On arrival, book guided 45-minute harbour tours for ages eight and up (included in admission) and whisper-boat harbour tours (*Apr-Oct; adult/child extra €6.50/4.50*).

Cruise Rotterdam's Harbour & Port with Royal Spido

BOAT TOUR

MAP: 11 P34 D7

Setting sail since 1919, **Koninklijke Spido** (*Royal Spido; spido.nl*) runs 75-minute harbour tours (*adult/child €17.50/9.80*) departing from Willemsplein, with awesome views of the skyscraper-filled skyline and ship-filled harbour, accompanied by multilingual commentary. There are up to 10 departures daily in July and August, fewer during the rest of the year.

At least one Saturday a month you can book a 2½-hour extended

PADDLING THROUGH THE CITY

Rotterdam might not be as woven with canals as many other Dutch cities, but there are still waterways to explore. Urban surfing hub **RiF010** rents SUPs (*stand-up paddleboards; per hour/half-day/full day €16/35/65*) and Canadian canoes carrying three adults or two adults and two children (*per hour/half-day/full day €17/40/75*), with life jackets provided, and has route advice. For an intrepid all-day adventure, you can paddle beneath the Hoogstraat to the Rotte – the Rhine-Maas-delta river dammed in 1270, giving the city its name. Paddling on, you can reach the Kralingse Plas lake in the **Kralingse Bos** and the Bergse Plassen, further north-west.

tour (*adult/child €29.50/17.25*) for closer views of the cranes, containers and precision shipping operations of Europe's biggest port.

To explore more of the port, on Tuesday and Saturday in July and August, all-day **Maasvlakte 2 harbour tours** (*adult/child incl lunch €67.95/38.95*) get you up next to massive 400m-long ships carrying upwards of 20,000 containers where wind turbines are built and giant crane-ships dock, and visit its state-of-the-art information centre, FutureLand, with interactive exhibits including VR and downloadable audio tours.

Alternatively, independent visits to **FutureLand** (*portofrotterdam.com; admission free, bus/boat port tours from €9.50/12.50*), 48km south-west of central Rotterdam, are possible with your own transport.

Immerse Yourself in 245 Million Pixels at Remastered GALLERY

MAP: 12 P34 D7

Below the Erasmusbrug, digital art is dazzling and interactive at **Remastered** (*remastered.nl; adult/family €24.50/75.50*), with a 'playground' where you can scan your image and create 3D art projected onto Europe's biggest indoor LED screen. A waterfall entrance and blackout passage with creatures by Hieronymus Bosch lead you to a fish-filled underwater world; next, you sail through bird- and cloud-filled skies to a garden of Eden, with a masterpiece-hung dollhouse and dramatic interpretations of works by Dutch artists such as Van Gogh and Mondrian. Wear comfortable shoes as there's no seating, although it's accessible for non-motorised wheelchairs. It's not suitable for anyone sensitive to intense light and sound, however, and kids must be aged over six.

Visits take an hour all up; book ahead online and arrive at least 15 minutes before your time slot. Afterwards, don't miss the city-skyline view from the terrace.

Ticket prices are steep, but there are combination deals with Koninklijke Spido (p49) 75-minute harbour tours (*adult/child €39.25/24.15*) and *SS Rotterdam* (p90) 90-minute ship tours (*€34/24.50*).

Climb the Laurenskerk's Medieval Tower CHURCH

MAP: 13 P34 D3

The city's only medieval structures to survive the 14 May 1940 bombing were the walls and tower of the Grote of Sint-Laurenskerk (Great Church or Church of St Lawrence), locally known as the **Laurenskerk** (*laurenskerkrotterdam.nl; church admission adult/child €4/free, tower €7.50/4.50*) or simply Laurens. The church was built between 1449 and 1525, becoming a Protestant church after the Reformation. Its restoration from 1952 to 1968 is testament to Rotterdam's determination and endurance; bronze door panels represent war and peace. Inside, the organs (including the Netherlands' largest, soaring 18m) can often be heard during concerts; check its website's schedule.

The church is open Tuesday to Saturday year-round (Sunday services are for worshippers only), but it's a popular events venue, so check ahead for closures. If you're fit, from March to October it's possible to climb the 63m-high tower's 367 steps past the 17th-century carillon to the roof for magnificent views over the city. Dates for guided tower tours are posted online (prior reservations aren't possible).

Check Out Rotterdam's Contemporary Art Scene at the Kunstblock

GALLERY

In vibrant art and nightlife quarter Witte de Withkwartier, centred on Witte de Withstraat, the Kunstblock (Art Block) brings together venues defining the contemporary artistic and cultural zeitgeist.

Within a former school, 1990-founded gallery **Kunstinstituut Melly** (MAP: 14 P34 **B5**; *kunstinstituutmelly.nl; adult/child €6/free*) has its finger on the pulse of contemporary art worldwide (its 2021 name change from the Witte de With Center for Contemporary Art was prompted by Dutch naval officer Witte de With's links to colonialism; its new name was inspired by Ken Lum's 1989 artwork *Melly Shum Hates Her Job* on its facade). Experimental exhibitions, installations and events often launch up-and-coming talent.

During Kunstavond events from 6pm to 9pm on Friday, admission to exhibitions and programs is free.

Other dynamic Kunstblock venues include young visual creators' hub **MaMA** (MAP: 15 P34 **B5**; *thisismama.nl*), interdisciplinary gallery **V2_** (MAP: 16 P34 **B5**; *v2.nl*), a 'Lab for the Unstable Media' with collaborations between scientists, software developers, artists and researchers; and one-of-a-kind hybrid **WORM** (MAP: 17 P34 **B5**; *worm.org*), a radical 'ultimate playground' for art in all its forms.

DUTCH FRIES, DECODED

Crispy, fluffy fries are among the Netherlands' favourite snacks. They're variously known as *Vlaamse frites* (Flemish fries), *friet*, *frieten* or *patat* (potatoes), depending on the region – in Rotterdam, friet is most common. Typically served in a paper cone with a small fork, they're either *zonder* (plain) or slathered with a choice of sauces. Mayonnaise is the default, but there are many other options. Popular local picks: *Pindasaus* (aka satésaus) peanut sauce. *Joppie* mixture of mayonnaise, ketchup and spices. *Oorlog* fiery peanut sauce, mayonnaise and raw chopped onions. *Curry spicy* curry sauce. *Stoofvlees* meat stew. *Kapsalon kebab* or shawarma and sometimes cheese.

Attend Sublime Performances Around Schouwburgplein

LIVE MUSIC

Renowned venues for Rotterdam's rich performing-arts scene concentrate around Schouwburgplein (*schouwburgpleinrotterdam.nl*).

The city's flagship **Theater Rotterdam** (MAP: 18 P34 **B3**; *TR; theaterrotterdam.nl*), has a changing calendar of dance, theatre and drama. Many performances are accessible for non-Dutch speakers, including plays in English, with subtitles or without spoken dialogue. Its main venue, at Schouwburgplein 25, seats 879 in its Grote Zaal (Great Hall) and 167 in its Kleine Zaal (Small Hall); separate Witte de Withstraat venue **TR8 William Boothlaan** (formerly the Ro Theater; MAP: 19 P34 **C5**) has a capacity of 250.

Concerts spanning classical, jazz and traditional music as well as pop, reggae and hip hop are held at **De Doelen** (MAP: 20 P34 **A2**; *dedoelen.nl*) at Schouwburgplein 50. Home venue of the acclaimed Rotterdams Philharmonisch Orkest (Rotterdam Philharmonic Orchestra), its Grote Zaal has 2190 seats and its Jurriaanse Zaal 587, with intimate gigs in its stage-less 180-seat Eduard Flipse Zaal.

Both new-release blockbusters and classic films play at the seven-screen **Pathé Cinema Schouwburgplein** (MAP: 21 P34 **A3**; *pathe.nl*), located at Schouwburgplein 101.

Schouwburgplein is a major hub during January/February's 11-day International Film Festival Rotterdam (*iffr.com*).

Find the Party

LIVE MUSIC, CLUB

Many Rotterdam nights out centre on **Annabel** (MAP: 22 P34 **B1**; *annabel.nu*), a brilliant midsized live-music venue hosting artists of all genres. Epic club nights take place on Friday and Saturday from 11pm to 4am; check the online agenda to find out what's coming up and to book tickets. From spring to autumn, its vast, 500-sq-metre cafe terrace often hosts events such as live bands, silent discos or salsa.

Another Rotterdam fixture is house and techno club Toffler (MAP: 23 P34 **B2**; *toffler.nl*), in an old tunnel near Centraal Station. It typically hosts events 11pm to 6am Friday and Saturday.

Best Places for...

€ Budget €€ Midrange €€€ Top End

See p34 for map of locations

Eating

Fries

Frietboutique €
 B5
Skin-on, agria-potato fries' classic toppings include mayo (with a vegan option) and peanut *satésaus*; it also serves truffle cheese, shrimp or vegetarian croquettes. *noon-10pm Sat-Thu, to 10.30pm Fri*

Pomms' €
 C3
Friet stand with organic, hand-cut, skin-on fries in cardboard cones with separate sauce compartments. *noon-8pm Wed, Thu, Sat & Sun, to 9pm Fri*

Schipper Patat €
 A2
Award-winning Frans Schipper has fried over half a million kilograms of potatoes in this spot near Centraal Station since 1979. *11am-5pm Wed-Sat, noon-5pm Sun*

Frites Unique €
 C8
Potato and sweet-potato fries with loaded toppings such as caramelised, soy-braised pork, piri-piri chicken or smoked-beef stew. *4-8pm Mon, noon-8pm Tue-Fri, 1-8pm Sat & Sun*

Cafes

Teds €€
 B1
Herbs, vegetables and honey harvested here on the rooftop of repurposed 1950s office building Schieblock are used in Teds' all-day brunch dishes. *10am-5pm Mon-Fri, 9am-5pm Sat & Sun*

RiF010 Surfbar & Kitchen €€
 D3
With views of the **urban surf** (p44), Rotterdam's only beach bar serves an all-day Mexican-inspired menu of pulled-pork or jackfruit tacos, cheese-smothered enchiladas and steak fajitas with *padrón* peppers. *9am-11pm*

Harvest Cafe & Bakery €€
 D5
All-day brunches (cornbread French toast with kimchi, *gochujang* hash browns with organic baked beans) and barista-world-champion-brewed coffee. *9am-4pm Mon & Wed-Fri, to 5pm Sat & Sun*

Fine Dining

Fred €€€
 E5
Fred Mustert's two-Michelin-star Art Deco–style dining room has a domed wine cellar, a climate-controlled cheese store and a heavenly cheese trolley. *noon-3pm & 6.30-10pm Mon, Tue, Thu & Fri, 6.30-10pm Sat*

Zeezout €€€
 B8
Michelin-star seafood specialist opposite the Nieuwe Maas; expect dishes such as salt-crusted sea bream, smoked-salmon profiteroles or tuna ceviche with oyster tartare and finger-lime sorbet. *noon-3pm & 6-10pm Wed-Sat*

Celest €€€

 C7

At research time, shortly to open atop the Netherlands' tallest building; its 'hot-air balloon to the moon' theme is based on an 1835 Edgar Allan Poe short story. *hours to be confirmed*

Burgers

Hamburg €

34 B5

Upstairs space (and street-side summer terrace) with burgers including triple cheese, brisket and vegan; classic, sweet-potato or loaded fries; and spiked milkshakes. *4-10pm Sun-Thu, to midnight Fri & Sat*

Ter Marsch & Co €€

see 24 B5

Former butcher shop with multiaward-winning burgers, including the Gojira (dry-aged ribeye, bulgogi pulled pork, kimchi and yuzu-and-ginger sauce); its fries are award winners, too. *10am-10pm*

Pizza

Old Scuola €€

 F2

In the restored 1952 Het Industriegebouw building now housing creative industries, with top-quality Neapolitan pizzas on pillowy bases. *5-11pm Mon-Thu, to midnight Fri*

O'Pazzo €€

 E2

Ingredients such as fresh ricotta, pancetta, *spianata calabra* (spiced salami), anchovies, olives and pine nuts are imported from Naples; desserts include homemade gelato and tiramisu. *11am-11pm*

La Pizza €€

 C7

Two-level restaurant with antipasti, 25 wood-fired pizzas (try the Tarantella, with black olives, nduja and burrata) and desserts (such as chocolate-and-pistachio-filled cannoli). *5.30-10pm Mon-Sat, to 9.30pm Sun*

Bakeries

Jan Bussing €

 C8

Baking breads including rye, buttermilk and spiced gingernut in a stone oven since 1899, with sandwiches and treats such as *hazelnoots chuimtaart* (hazelnut meringue cake). *8am-5pm Mon-Fri, to 3pm Sat*

SUE €

 E1

Dates, rice syrup and coconut blossom replace refined sugar at this vegan, lactose- and gluten-free bakery in treats such as lemon-and-lavender slice and raspberry cheesecake. *8am-4pm Mon-Fri, 9am-4pm Sat*

Bas Bakt €

 C5

Eight handcrafted sourdoughs and buttery croissants are used in sandwiches and toasties to eat at its sociable tables or sunny terrace or to take away. *8am-4pm Mon-Sat*

Ice Cream

De IJsmaker €

 C5

Artisanal ice cream using only quality produce (such as pistachio nuts from Sicily and vanilla beans from Madagascar). There are branches in West and Noord. *noon-11pm*

Amy's Frozen Yoghurt €

42 E3

In Markthal, serving natural Dutch yoghurt from local sustainable farms topped with fresh fruit, gluten-free granola, toasted nuts or *stroopwafel* crumbs. *10am-8pm Mon-Sat, to 6pm Sun*

Capri IJssalon €

43 B3

Real Italian gelato since 1957; daily changing flavours (including lactose- and gluten-free options) might feature tiramisu, chocolate amaretto or limoncello; there are also ice-cream cakes and milkshakes. *noon-midnight*

Asian

Sojubar ❸

 B5

Korean crispy double-fried chicken, *bibimbap* (rice bowls) and steamed *mandu* (dumplings), along with Korean beer and *soju* (sweet Korean rice spirit). *noon-9.30pm Sun-Thu, to 10pm Fri & Sat*

Yellow River ❸❸

 A4

Watch traditional Lanzhou noodles being hand-pulled in the open kitchen before they're served steamed, wok-fried, braised or in soup. *noon-8.30pm*

Asian Glories ❸❸

 D3

Family-recipe Cantonese and Sichuan dishes span steamed scallops with glass noodles, Peking duck pancakes, and crispy beef with mandarin sweet-and-sour sauce. *noon-10pm Mon & Thu-Sat, to 9pm Sun*

Kyatcha ❸❸❸

 D6

Modern Japanese in the Leuvepaviljoen might serve soy-poached eel with daikon or charcoal-grilled wagyuwith truffle *ponzu* dressing. *5-11pm Sun, Tue & Wed, to midnight Thu-Sat*

Drinking

Wine Bars

Verward

 F2

Sommelier Ward de Zeeuw pours 50 biodynamic wines; there are also more than 30 Dutch and Belgian beers. *3-9pm Mon, to 11pm Tue-Thu, to midnight Fri, 2pm-midnight Sat, 1-8pm Sun*

LenselinQ Wijnimport

 C2

Natural and organic wines sourced directly from small-scale vineyards in Sardinia, Sicily, Corsica, Majorca and Malta. *4-9pm Thu & Fri, 2-9pm Sat, to 6pm Sun*

Beer

Biergarten

see 28 B1

Sunny courtyard next to the Luchtsingel strewn with picnic tables; beers are served in steins. *3pm-midnight Mon-Thu, to 1am Fri, noon-1am Sat, noon-midnight Sun*

Bokaal

 E2

Bokaal's 11 taps and 80-plus bottles include rare Trappist beers and local Rotterdam brews such as Stadshaven's Piranha tripel, Reijgoud's sour, and Kaapse Brouwers' Karel gluten-free IPA. *11am-1am*

Bier Boutique

 C5

Witte de Withstraat bar with gold walls and velvet chairs; 90 beers and ciders, including 10 rotating on the taps. *4pm-1am Wed, to 4am Wed-Sat, 1pm-1am Sun*

De Kerktuin

 B5

Opposite the Westersingel in the forecourt of 1897 Arminiuskerk with more than 60 bottled beers. *5pm-midnight Tue-Thu, 2pm-1am Fri, noon-1pm Sat, 1pm-midnight Sun, closed Dec-Feb & in bad weather*

Cocktails

Ballroom

 B5

With more than 160 gins and 12 tonics, Ballroom can mix almost 2000 G&T combinations. There's a leafy summer beer garden. *4pm-1am Thu & Sun, to 2am Fri & Sat*

Spikizi

 C5

Homemade infusions and syrups in a narrow 'speakeasy' off Witte de Withstraat. *5pm-1am*

Sun & Tue-Thu, to 2am Fri & Sat

Rumah

55 B4

This rum specialist's cocktails include Rumboo Colada (strawberries and pink pepper) and 40 Pounds (lychee liqueur and grapefruit). *5pm-1am Mon, Wed & Thu, to 2am Fri, 2pm-2am Sat, 2pm-1am Sun*

160K

 B1

Retro arcade bar with pinball machines and video games, and themed cocktails such as the Double Dragon Dutch Martini and the Bloody Pacman. *5pm-1am Wed & Thu, to 2am Fri & Sat*

Coffee

Giraffe Coffee Bar & Academy

 F2

Supplying cafes across the Netherlands, this Rotterdam roastery's flagship showcases its blends every which way: V60, AeroPress, cold brew and pour-over. Also runs coffee-art and barista courses. *8am-5pm*

Dune

 B7

A collaboration between Rotterdam roastery Shokunin Coffee and kombucha brewery BAIN Brewing, this minimalist space has 15 coffee blends complete with tasting notes. *8am-4pm Mon-Fri, 9am-5pm Sat & Sun*

Hopper Coffee

 C5

Industrial-style cafe roasting its own coffee using single-source beans and offering both espresso and AeroPress styles, with its own on-site bakery. *8.30am-5.30pm Mon-Fri, 9.30am-5.30pm Sat & Sun*

Crave Coffee & Bakery

60 E2

Coffee and loose-leaf teas from Rotterdam's Tea Lab come with oat, almond or pea-protein milk at this vegan cafe, with treats including chocolate babka. *9am-4pm Tue-Sun*

Shopping

Department Stores & Malls

De Bijenkorf

 C3

Upmarket 1957-opened department store designed by Bauhaus architect Marcel Breuer; its name ('the beehive') is reflected in its honeycomb-like cladding. *10am-8pm Tue-Thu & Sat, 10am-9pm Fri, 11am-7pm Sun, 11am-8pm Mon*

De Groene Passage

 E2

'Green' arcade of sustainable small businesses (eco-design shop, natural beauty salon, green supermarket, organic artisan butcher, plus a vegan restaurant, Sprit, and a cocktail bar, Botanero). *hours vary*

Beurstraverse (Koopgoot)

63 C4

Stretching 300m below street level between Rodezand and Hennekijnstraat, this 1996-completed, glass-canopied open-air mall dubbed the 'shopping trench' has 80 high-street chains (eg Hema) and pop-ups. *hours vary*

Lijnbaan

64 B3

Built in 1953, Lijnbaan was Europe's first purpose-built car-free shopping street; fashion chains include Wam Denim, Pull & Bear clothing, Jacobs Rotterdam menswear and Vans shoes. *hours vary*

Dutch Fashion

Very Cherry

 E2

Designer Caroline Poiesz' 1940s- to '60s-inspired pieces in natural materials are stocked alongside retro labels such as Lindy Bop, Esther Williams Swimwear and Pinup Couture. *10am-6pm Tue-Sat, noon-5pm Sun*

Wendela van Dijk

 A4

High-end boutique with womenswear, footwear, accessories and jewellery from local designers such as Susan Bijl, Monique van Heist and Christian Wijnants. *10am-6pm Tue-Sat, 1-5pm Sun & Mon*

Devastator

67 B4

Founded by Dutch designers Arij den Otter and Erik Bosman, who use leftover fabric to create their own pieces and stock similar ethically minded labels. *10am-6pm Tue-Sat, 1-6pm Sun*

Chocolate

Chocoholic

68 F2

Chocolatier Marco Harreman uses ingredients such as sea buckthorn and hibiscus blossom in bonbons and bars (including vegan options). Don't miss the deliciously rich spiced hot chocolate. *9am-5pm Tue-Sat*

Coco & Sebas

 C3

Rainforest Alliance cocoa is used in handcrafted truffles, tulips, Dutch houses and delftware. *10am-6pm Tue-Thu & Sat, to 9pm Fri, noon-6pm Sun & Mon*

Chocolate Company

70 B4

Dutch-inspired flavours include *stroopwafel*, cinnamon and ginger, *jenever* (traditional gin), and Dutch breakfast favourite chocolate sprinkles; its cafe serves chocolate fondue. *9am-6pm Mon-Fri, to 7pm Sat, 10am-6pm Sun*

See p66
for eating, drinking and shopping listings

Explore Noord

Bordering Centrum to the south, linked by the Luchtsingel ('air canal'), Noord is rapidly becoming one of Rotterdam's most exciting neighbourhoods, with redevelopments around the Netherlands' longest listed monument, the Hofbogen, the viaduct of the former Hofpleinlijn that until only recently carried rail services to Den Haag. Now its arches and former stations house creative enterprises, while an elevated park is being created on top. And it's not all urban here: numerous other green spaces in Noord include the city's conservation-driven zoo, Diergaarde Blijdorp; the adjacent Vroesenpark, Trompenburg's glorious botanic gardens and arboretum; and the grassland and woodland of rambling Kralingse Bos.

Getting Around

Walk

Noord is easily reached via Centraal's northern exit or by crossing the Lutchsingel footbridge from Centrum's north-eastern corner.

Metro

Lines A, B and C stop at Voorschoterlaan and Kralingse Zoom, close to Kralingse Bos. Line E serves Blijdorp in Noord's north-eastern corner, near the Diergaarde Blijdorp zoo, en route to Den Haag.

Tram

Lines 4, 7 and 8 cover Noord's north-eastern area. Line 25 (direction Schiebroek) serves the north-west.

THE BEST

LAKE
Kralingse Plas (p61)

JAZZ CLUB
Bird (p64)

STEAM TRAIN COLLECTION
Stoom Stichting Nederland (p61)

PARK PICNIC
Vroesenpaviljoen (p64)

FOOD HALL
Station Bergweg (p66)

Luchtsingel (p63)
CHENPROJECT/SHUTTERSTOCK ©

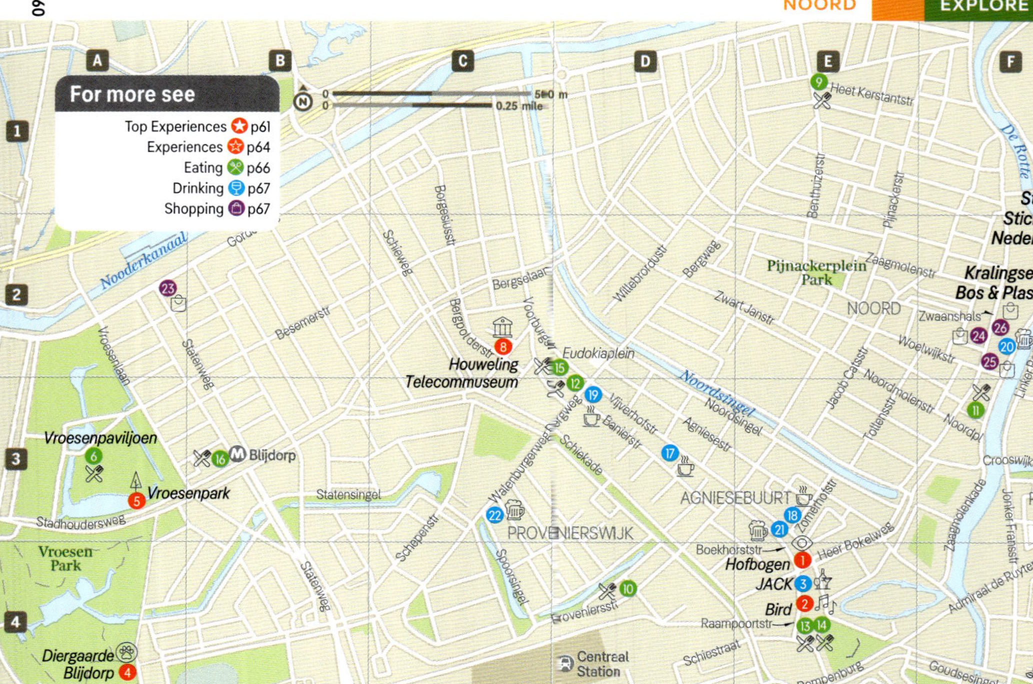
For more see
Top Experiences p61
Experiences p64
Eating p66
Drinking p67
Shopping p67
500 m
0.25 mile
Vroesenpaviljoen
Vroesenpark
Vroesen Park
Diergaarde Blijdorp
Blijdorp
Houweling Telecommuseum
Eudokiaplein
Stoom Stichting Nederland
Kralingse Bos & Plas
Pijnackerplein Park
NOORD
AGNIESEBUURT
PROVENIERSWIJK
RUBROEK
Hofbogen
JACK
Bird
Centraal Station
De Rotte
Noorderkanaal
Noordsingel
Heet Kerstantstr
Benthuizerstr
Pijnackerstr
Zaagmolenstr
Zwaanshals
Woelwijkstr
Linker Rottekade
Noordmolenstr
Noordpl
Jacob Catsstr
Tollensstr
Crooswijksesingel
Zaagmolenkade
Jonker Fransstr
Admiraal de Ruyterweg
Goudsesingel
Pompenburg
Schiestraat
Raampoortstr
Boekhorststr
Heer Bokelweg
Zomerhofstr
Agniesestr
Banierstr
Vijverhofstr
Schiekade
Walenburgerweg
Spoorsingel
Provenierssstr
Schepenstr
Statensingel
Statenweg
Stadhoudersweg
Vroesenlaan
Besemerstr
Bergpolderstr
Bergselaan
Voorburgstr
Borgesiusstr
Schieweg
Willebrordusstr
Bergweg
Zwart Janstr

★ TOP EXPERIENCE

Kralingse Bos Forest

Bucolic Kralingse Bos – Rotterdam's largest park at around 250 hectares – sprawls just outside the centre. It offers an idyllic blend of cool, shaded forest; sunny grassy areas; and the sparkling waters of its centrepiece lake, Kralingse Plas, with activities including water sports, golf and horse riding.

MAP **F2**

Park History & Layout

Covering 100 hectares, square-shaped Kralingse Plas was created in the 17th century after peat was extracted here. Historic snuff-and-spice windmills De Ster and De Lelie (*snuifmolens.nl; 10am-4.30pm Wed, Thu & Sat; free*) spin on the lake's south-western edge. Polder (drained land) was built after 1895, and the first tree was planted in 1928. WWII rubble dumped in the lake's southern corner created islands, linked by walkways.

Activities & Refreshments

Cycling and walking paths lace the park; the 5km walk around the lake takes about an hour. Kids love the playgrounds, petting zoo and 'fun forest' climbing park. Sailing and canoeing are popular, and swimming is possible May to October. Festivals are held in the warmer months.

Cafes include forest-set **Pannekoekhuis De Nachtegaal** and lakeside **De Schone Lei** and **Beach House**.

Steam Train Centre

Just outside the park, **Stoom Stichting Nederland** (*stoomstichting.nl; 10am-3pm Wed, to 5pm Sat; adult/child €5/3*) houses model railways and steam locomotives and runs train rides on events days. Watch volunteers restoring the trains in the workshop.

PLANNING TIP
Ideally explored by bike, Kralingse Bos is some 4km northeast of Noord. Cycling takes around 15 minutes from Rotterdam Centraal Station, or you can take tram 7 from Centraal to Voorschoterlaan.

Scan for opening hours and other information.

Walk Noord

On this stroll the cityscape rises three-dimensionally from the streets below. Starting on the footbridge that in recent years has reconnected the neighbourhood with the city centre gives you a bird's eye view of the transformation taking place on, around and above the Hofbogen viaduct of the former Hofpleinlijn railway line before you meander Noord's peaceful canals.

START	END	LENGTH
Luchtsingel (tram 7/8 Pompenburg)	Spoorsingel (metro Centraal Station)	3km; 2 hours

1 Air Canal

Begin on the bright-yellow, 400m-long **Luchtsingel** linking Centrum with Noord. This elevated pedestrian bridge, opened in 2015, was designed by local studio ZUS and funded by a crowdsourcing campaign (a world-first for public infrastructure); look for the names inscribed in the wooden panels.

2 Air Park

The Luchtsingel takes you onto the 2018-opened **Luchtpark Hofbogen**, the rooftop garden of the former Hofpleinlijn's Rotterdam terminus, Station Hofplein. Open from 8.30am to 6pm, this 'air park' is a Rotterdamse Dakendagen (*Rotterdam Rooftop Days; rotterdamsedakendagen.nl*) location each May, and will connect to the upcoming Hofbogenpark (p65). Descending the southern staircase, look for the station's changing street-art-painted wall.

3 Neighbourhood Square

Head east to Rotterdam's namesake waterway, the Rotte. Follow its left bank to large public square **Noordplein**. On Saturday it's home to the Oogstmarkt (*rotterdamseoogst.nl*) farmers market, with around 50 stalls selling artisan produce and crafts produced within a 50km radius. Late June's Rotterdam Bluegrass Festival (*bluegrassfestival.nl*) sees three stages, a jam area, workshops, theatre and street-food stalls occupy the square.

4 Canal Architecture

Walk west from Noordplein along the Noordsingel canal. You'll pass architect Willem Cornelis Metzelaar's 1898-built **courthouse** (housing offices since 1996). It's in front of the Gevangenis Noordsingel, a prison dating from 1866 (designed by Metzelaar's father) that became a housing complex in 2018.

5 Food Hall

Continue north-west along Noordsingel to the Hofbogen's **Station Bergweg** (*stationbergweg.nl*), another former Hofpleinlijn station. It was transformed in 2021 into a fabulous food hall with a dozen stalls spanning *pintxos* to hot dogs, smash burgers and craft beer Wednesday to Sunday.

6 Canal Art

From Station Bergweg, walk south-west along the pretty Spoorsingel canal. To the east you'll see the Provenierssingel canal, while at the Spoorsingel's southern end on a small island you'll spot artist Henk Visch's 2013 bronze sculpture, the open-armed **De Jonge Mens Op Het Eiland** (*The Young Man on the Island*), embracing the surrounding water and the city. Footsteps south, a tunnel leads to Centraal Station.

EXPERIENCES

Visit a Viaduct District ARCHITECTURE, LIVE MUSIC

Beneath the **Hofbogen** (MAP: 1 P60 **E4**) at street level, the viaduct's arches now house cafes, restaurants, a food hall complete with pinball machines (in the former Station Bergweg, p66), shops and creative spaces. One of the liveliest, at the former **Station Hofplein**, is **Bird** (MAP: 2 P60 **E4**; *bird-rotterdam.nl*), named for saxophonist Charlie 'Bird' Parker, and hosting live jazz, soul, hip-hop, funk and electronica, as well as July's North Sea Jazz Festival's official afterparty, the BoogieBall. Its restaurant specialises in wood-fired pizzas; the Garden of Bird terrace opens from April to mid October. Nearby, neon-lit restaurant-cocktail bar **JACK** (MAP: 3 P60 **E4**; *jack-rotter*) revolves around electronica and house music.

Meet Endangered Animals ZOO

MAP: 4 P60 **A4**

Conserving endangered animals and their global habitats and preventing extinction are vital to **Diergaarde Blijdorp** (*diergaardeblijdorp.nl; adult/child from €27.50/22.50*), one of the Netherlands' oldest zoos, founded in 1857. Across 34 hectares you can explore the challenges, impact and goals of its diverse environments, including East African savannah (home to giraffes, zebras and black rhinos), central and West African rainforest (with species including pygmy hippos, okapis, and bongos), Asian 'corridors' (with lions, Sumatran tigers and Asian elephants), Himalayan peaks (Indian rhinos, red pandas and tufted deer) and North Sea and tropical Caribbean coast aquariums (where sharks and sea turtles swim around you), as well as natural Dutch landscapes. Together, they're home to 5600 individual animal and plant species.

Downloading the Blijdorp app helps plan your day (including animal feeding times). For lunch, there are numerous family-oriented restaurants and snack bars. Tickets are cheaper online or you can buy them when you arrive (time slots aren't required); the main entrance is at Blijdorplaan 8.

Unwind in the Vroesenpark PARK

Directly opposite Rotterdam's Diergaarde Blijdorp zoo, accessed along Vroesenlaan, the **Vroesenpark** (MAP: 5 P60 **A3**) sprawls over 9.8 hectares. Created in 1929 as an ornamental garden, it was redesigned as a public park in 1948 and named in 1977 for the Vroesen family of former Rotterdam mayors. Its expansive lawns, walking paths and ponds make it a peaceful place to kick back, with playgrounds for kids and areas for picnicking.

In the centre of the park, the **Vroesenpaviljoen** (MAP: 6 P60 **A3**; *vroesenpaviljoen.nl*) is a great spot to pick up takeaway coffees, pastries, or lunch dishes such as soups, sandwiches and salads made from locally sourced ingredients. You can also dine on-site outdoors or in the pavilion on breakfast (eggs, blueberry pancakes, chia-seed pudding), lunch or bar snacks during *borrel* ('drinks'). The Vroesenpaviljoen hosts regular events, with festivals setting up here in warmer months.

Explore Tranquil Trompenburg

GARDENS

MAP: 7 P60 F4

Picturesque in all seasons, Rotterdam's 'Green Museum', 1820-established former country estate **Trompenburg Gardens & Arboretum** (*trompenburg.nl; adult/child €11/2.50*) is adjacent to the Erasmus University Rotterdam in Kralingen. Within this 8-hectare oasis, walking paths wind around tree-, shrub- and flower-filled gardens, including Dutch national collections of oak, beech and holly, and some 700 rhododendron varieties ablaze with colour in spring, along with a desert-climate hothouse filled with succulents and a re-created forest of edible plants, that have given Trompenburg museum and municipal monument status. Seasonal activities include themed routes such as caterpillars and butterflies, classical music, plant markets and a Christmas market.

With tables encircled by foliage, its charming restaurant, Flora, serves coffee, high tea and set lunches (you'll need a ticket to the gardens). It's an easy cycle (around 15 minutes from Centraal Station; less from Noord's eastern edge), or take tram 21 or 24 from Centraal (direction De Esch) to Woudestein.

See Historic Phone Equipment

MUSEUM

MAP: 8 P60 C2

In Noord's 1923-built, still-operating telephone exchange, the **Houweling Telecommuseum** (*houwelingtelecommuseum.nl; admission free*) is niche but fascinating if you're interested in the evolution of telecoms. Displays include old and modern phones, phone boxes, telephone exchanges, faxes, radios, cables and more, all in working order. Staffed by former telecom employees, it's only open on Tuesday from 9.30am to 4pm; 90-minute guided tours are available.

CREATING THE HOFBOGENPARK

Stretching atop the 8m-high viaduct of the Hofpleinlijn – the Netherlands' first electric railway line, built between 1904 and 1908, last trains ran in 2010 – the **Hofbogenpark** (*rotterdam.nl/hofbogenpark*) will be the country's longest (2km) and narrowest (6m) elevated park. Accessed by staircases and elevators, with benches, platforms, ponds and play areas, the sustainable rooftop park will collect and purify rainwater for trees, plants and fragrant flowers, creating a habitat for bees, butterflies, bats, birds and hedgehogs. Construction starts in 2025; it will open in stages before its end-of-2027 completion. Ultimately the goal is a bridge over the A20, forming part of a larger green network.

LISTINGS

Best Places for...

€ Budget €€ Midrange €€€ Top End

See p60 for map of locations

Eating

Wine-Bar Dining

Diepnoord €€

9 E1

Candlelit tables create an elegant setting for chef Rokus de Jong's weekly changing menu of shared plates such as seared tuna and kiwifruit. *5.30-10pm Thu-Mon*

Le Nord €€

 D4

Organic ingredients from within a 15km radius are used in Dutch-French dishes and charcuterie platters; 50-plus beers and 70-plus natural wines. *5-10pm Mon & Tue, noon-2.30pm & 5-10pm Wed-Sun*

Fermin €€

 F3

Natural wines pair with the daily six-course chef's menu of nose-to-tail dishes in this small restaurant on the Noordplein. *6-10pm Wed-Sat*

Hofbogen Dining

Station Bergweg €

 D3

Opened in a century-old train station in 2024, with 11 bars and eateries and a roof-terrace summer cinema. *noon-10pm Wed-Sat, to 9pm Sun*

Roosje €€

 E4

Under the Luchtpark, with twists on *borrel-hapjes* (bar snacks) such as chorizo croquettes, peanut-crusted chicken skewers and vegan *bitter-ballen*. *3-9.30pm Tue-Thu, 3-10.30pm Fri, 1-10.30pm Sat & Sun, closed Aug*

Franky's Grill €€

14 E4

François Geurds (aka FG) is one of Rotterdam's most interesting and experimental chefs. This casual bistro offers barbecue grills; FG's two-Michelin-star flagship is next door. *6-8.30pm Wed-Fri, 2-8.30pm Sat, 3-8.30pm Sun*

Bakeries

Urban Bakery €

 D2

Watch all-natural treats such as pistachio-and-apricot slices and mini cheesecakes being baked at this Hofbogen viaduct favourite. *10am-5pm Mon, 8.30am-5pm Tue-Sat, 10am-3pm Sun*

Jordy's €

see  F3

Artisan sourdoughs span walnut and raisin, pumpkin, hazelnut and fig, and more, with sweeter treats including blackcurrant muffins and raspberry brownies, plus family-recipe *speculaas* (spiced biscuits) in December. *8am-6pm*

Banketbakkerij €

 B3

Next to Blijdorp metro station; sells traditional Dutch treats such as *stroopwafels* (caramel-syrup-sandwiched waffles), *poffertjes* (mini pancakes), and *oliebollen* (doughnuts). *8.30am-5.30pm Wed-Sat*

Drinking

Coffee

Man Met Bril Koffie

17 D3

Artisan space sourcing direct-trade, organic beans from around the globe and roasting them at its minimalist, plant-filled cafe under the Hofbogen. *7am-5pm Mon-Fri, 8am-6pm Sat & Sun*

Bonza Koffie

18 E3

Iced V60 drip coffees, chai and pumpkin lattes and melon matchas, plus classic brews and loose-leaf teas. Great food includes goats cheese toasties and banana bread. *8am-3.30pm Mon-Fri*

COPPI

19 D3

Cafe and bike repairer; screens major cycling races and holds cycling tours on the first Sunday of the month (10am; all welcome; helmets compulsory). *8.30am-5pm Mon-Fri, 9.30am-5pm Sat & Sun*

Breweries

Brouwerij Noordt

20 F2

In an old fire station, with tanks in its 20-tap tasting room; ask about 30-minute tours in English (€13.50 including 2 tastings). *2-7pm Sun & Thu, to 9pm Fri & Sat*

Brewpub Reijngoud

21 E3

Brews 10 beers here and carries another 200 Dutch varieties. *3pm-1am Thu, 3pm-2am Fri & Sat, noon-1pm Sun*

De Hoevebrugsche Bierbrouwerij

22 C3

On the Spoorsingel, this is the Netherlands' smallest fully operational brewery, grinding its own malt and labelling its own bottles. *6-11pm Tue & Thu*

Shopping

Vintage

Kringloopwinkel

23 A2

A treasure hunt through haphazardly stacked clothing, furniture, whitegoods, records, bric-a-brac and curios. Look for the Roman centurion statue out the front. *10am-5pm Mon-Sat*

CENO

24 F2

In the Zwaanshals area with numerous vintage shops; sustainable boutique focusing on natural materials, neutral colour palettes and high-quality pieces such as trench coats. *11am-6pm Wed-Sat*

Vintage aan de Rotte

25 F2

Super-cool boutique specialising in 60s and 70s Dutch homewares such as retro vases, lamps, rugs, furniture and electrical goods like radios. *11am-5pm Wed-Sat*

Music

Clone

see 3 E4

Dutch experimental/underground electronic-dance-music record label and vinyl shop with thousands of titles plus hard-to-find merch. *10.30am-6pm Mon-Thu & Sat, 10.30-9pm Fri, noon-5pm Sun*

Offbeat Records

see 24 F2

Popular with Rotterdam DJs for dance-oriented vinyl covering disco, wave, house, techno, electro and jungle, among other genres. *noon-7pm Thu, to 9pm Fri, to 6pm Sat*

JensDoRecords

26 F2

LPs of all genres, with an wide-ranging selection of jazz and bluegrass, and vintage record players. *noon-5pm Wed-Fri, 11am-5.30pm Sat*

See p81
for eating,
drinking and
shopping
listings

Explore West

Stretching immediately south-west of Centraal Station, this sprawling neighbourhood is home to landmarks such as the Euromast, UNESCO site and spectacular former factory Van Nelle Fabriek, and the city's most moving museum, the Museum Rotterdam '40-'45 NU, which recalls WWII's harrowing bombardments. West also has wonderful green spaces such as Het Park, and lively cafe and restaurant strips including Nieuwe Binnenweg. Further west, historic buildings include windmills in the enclaves of Delfshaven, from where the Pilgrims set sail for America, and Schiedam, a 17th-century production centre of *jenever* (traditional Dutch gin), with museums, distilleries and charming cafes for tastings.

Getting Around

Metro

Lines A, B and C serve West; all three run to Schiedam. Major stops include Eendrachtsplein, Dijkzigt (for Het Park and the Euromast), Delfshaven, Marconiplein and Schiedam Centrum.

Tram

Line 4 runs along Nieuwe Binnenweg to Heemraadsplein. Line 8 runs along Westzeedijk via Het Park and Delfshaven to Marconiplein. Lines 21, 23 and 24 travel west along Middellandstraat; lines 21 and 24 continue to Schiedam.

Ferry

There are watertaxi stops at Sint Jobshaven and Schiemond, both at Delfshaven, and Keilehaven, and at Marconistraat, near Marconiplein.

Delfshaven

ALEKSANDAR VRZALSKI/GETTY IMAGES ©

THE BEST

ARCHITECTURAL TOUR Van Nelle Fabriek (p72)

VIEWS Euromast (p78)

JENEVER MUSEUM Nationaal Jenevermuseum Schiedam (p80)

WINDMILL Korenmolen de Walvisch (p80)

MODEL RAILROAD Miniworld Rotterdam (p78)

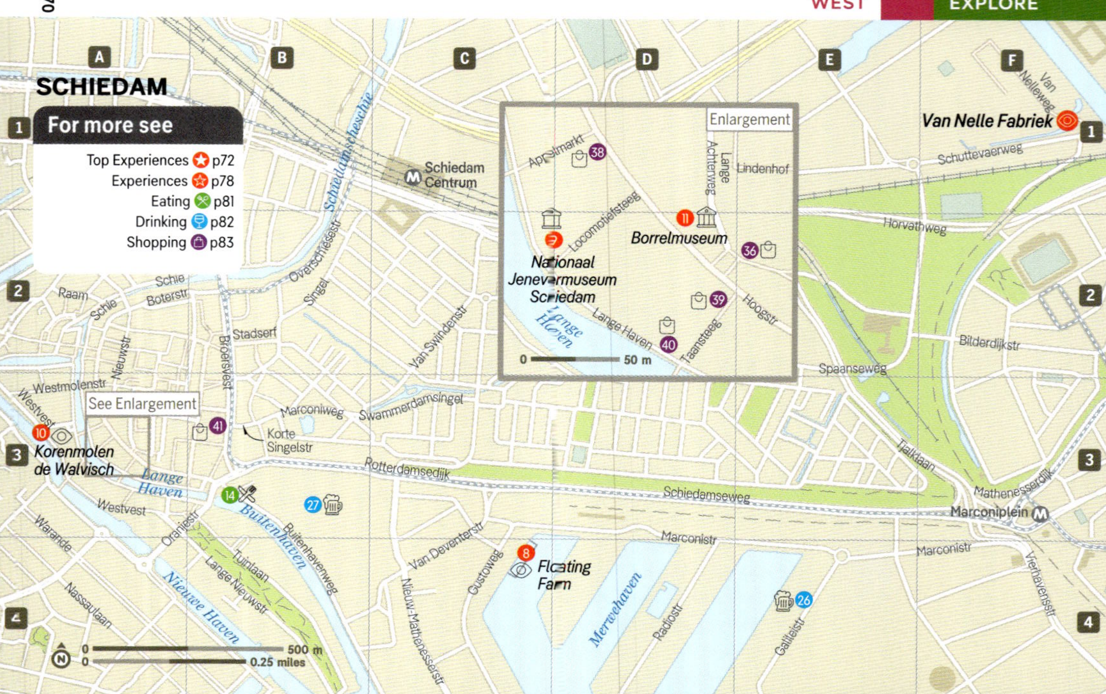
SCHIEDAM
For more see
Top Experiences p72
Experiences p78
Eating p81
Drinking p82
Shopping p83
Van Nelle Fabriek
Schiedam Centrum
Enlargement
See Enlargement
Borrelmuseum
Nationaal Jenevermuseum Schiedam
Korenmolen de Walvisch
Floating Farm
Schiedamsche Schie
Overschiesestr
Singel
Van Swindenstr
Swammerdamsingel
Marconiweg
Korte Singelstr
Rotterdamsedijk
Schiedamseweg
Marconiplein
Marconistr
Mathenesserdijk
Vierhavensstr
Tjalklaan
Spaanseweg
Bilderdijkstr
Horvathweg
Schuttevaerweg
Van Nelleweg
Aprilmarkt
Lange Achterweg
Lindenhof
Locomotiefsteeg
Lange Haven
Taansteeg
Hoogstr
Raam
Schie
Boterstr
Stadserf
Broersvest
Nieuwstr
Westmolenstr
Westvest
Warande
Nassaulaan
Oranjestr
Tuinlaan
Lange Nieuwstr
Nieuwe Haven
Buitenhaven
Buitenhavenweg
Van Deventerstr
Nieuw-Mathenesserstr
Gustoweg
Merwehaven
Radiostr
Galileistr
0 50 m
0 500 m
0 0.25 miles

DELFSHAVEN

A B C D
1 2 3 4 5 6

Centraal Station
Stationspl
Centraal
30
Miniworld Rotterdam 2
Roel Langerak Park
Beukelsdijk
Beukelsdijk
Hennegouwerlaan
Kruispl
West Kruiskade
OUDE WESTEN
Gouvernestr
Westersingel
Mauritsweg
V Citersstr
Aleidisstr
Aleidisstr
1e Middellandstr
18
33 20
17 37
34 Nieuwe Binnenweg
Vierambachtsstr
MIDDELLAND
Heemraadssingel
's- Gravendijkwal
Mathenesserlaan
NIEUWE WESTEN
Albrechtskade
Spanjaardstr
Delfshavense Schie
Mathenesserlaan
Volmarijnstr
24
19 31
Rochussenstr
Museumpark
Westzeedijk
12
35
Nieuwe Binnenweg
Dijkzigt
DIJKZIGT
Schiedam (2.5km)
Mathenesserdijk
Delfshaven
13
Heemraadssingel
Rochussenstr
's- Gravendijkwal
Havenstraat
28
Aelbrechtskolk
Rochussenstr
Coolhaven
Coolhaven
Museum Rotterdam '40-'45 NU
21
Historische Tuin Schoonoord 5
25
Achterwater
Coolhaven
7
Piet Heynsplein
23
6
TENT
29
Westzeedijk
Kievitslaan
Dudok in Het Park
Dutch Pinball Museum 15
Willem Buytewechstr
LLOYDKWARTIER
4
Voorhaven
Achterhaven
DELFSHAVEN
Helman Dullaertplein
Parkhaven
Parkhaven
Euromast 1
3
Het Park
22
Vierhavensstr
Middenkous
Sint-Jobsweg
Westzeedijk
Lloydstr
Maastunnel
5
SCHIEMOND
Schiehavenweg
Schiehaven
1e Middellandstr
Parkkade
32
16

For more see

Top Experiences p72
Experiences p78
Eating p81
Drinking p82
Shopping p83

0 500 m
0 0.25 miles

★ TOP EXPERIENCE

Van Nelle Fabriek

One of only 12 World Heritage-listed sights in the Netherlands, this former coffee, tea and tobacco factory, built between 1925 and 1931, is a gleaming triumph of modernist architecture. It is widely acknowledged to be one of the global icons of 20th-century industrial architecture.

MAP P70 **F1**

PLANNING TIP
The factory can only be visited on Saturday-afternoon tours led by Urban Guides in conjunction with the **Chabot Museum**, with tickets including Chabot admission or private Urban Guides tours.

Scan this QR code for opening hours and information on booking.

The Architectural Vision

Conceived as an 'ideal factory' where interior working spaces evolved according to need and where daylight was used to provide healthy and enjoyable (and therefore productive) working conditions, the factory became a symbol of interwar modernity as soon as it opened.

Architects Johannes Brinkman and Leendert van der Vlugt, Rotterdam-based exponents of the Nieuwe Bouwen (Dutch Functionalist) movement, designed a streamlined concrete structure sheathed in a massive curtain wall of glass and steel that has seen the edifice dubbed the 'glass palace'.

Brinkman and Van der Vlugt also designed Huis Sonneveld (p36), adjacent to Museumpark in Centrum, as a family home for Albertus Sonneveld, a company director at Van Nelle.

Renowned Swiss-French International School of Architecture visionary Le Corbusier, whose designs also combined functionalism with sculptural expressionism, was a fan of Van Nelle Fabriek, describing it as the 'most beautiful spectacle of the modern age'.

Notable Features

The factory's three main sections – one for tobacco, one for coffee and one for tea – are linked with service areas containing washrooms, stairs and lifts. All three are connected by distinctive elevated bridges.

Within the factory complex there is an office building whose sinuous form mirrors the curve of the entrance driveway, a circular tea room on top of

TTSTOCK/SHUTTERSTOCK ©

the tobacco section, separate male and female staircases (to prevent staff fraternisation) and an on-site electricity plant. The factory operated until the 1990s and now houses creative industries.

From the factory gate, by the porter's lodge, one-hour guided walking tours (in English) from 3pm to 4pm on Saturday afternoons (book ahead; adult/child €19.50/12.50) take in the factory's architecture, former production process and its preservation.

Outside the Factory

The Van Nelle Fabriek stands on the banks of the Delfshavense Schie canal in Rotterdam's inner northwest. The low orange-and-blue bunker to the east of the factory is the De Schie Penitentiary, designed by CJM Weeber and constructed between 1985 and 1989. Its startlingly vivid colour scheme is in stark contrast to its dark function.

QUICK BREAK

Walk south along the canal to historic Delfshaven, where you can enjoy a beer at brewery **Stadsbrouwerij De Pelgrim** (p82) or *borrelhapjes* (bar snacks) at charming **De Oude Sluis** (p82).

★ TOP EXPERIENCE

Museum Rotterdam '40-'45 NU

Sheltered under a bridge on Coolhaven, this small, powerful museum documents life in Rotterdam in WWII, outlining the terror and destruction caused by the bombardment of the city on 14 May 1940, when 54 German aircraft dropped 1300 bombs over a 13-minute period.

MAP P71 **C4**

PLANNING TIP
The museum is closed on Monday. Admission is free on the first Wednesday of each month. In spring especially, weekdays can get busy with school groups.

Scan this QR code for full opening hours and information on booking.

The Exhibitions

The Museum Rotterdam '40-'45 NU (*adult/child €10/free*) gives you a sense of life in Rotterdam before 14 May 1940, with multimedia, recovered objects and personal experiences putting WWII's devastating events into human context. Its second location in the Timmerhuis, in Centrum, closed in 2020; a new general location is planned in the future.

The immersive multimedia experience gives you a vivid insight into the seismic effects of the bombardment of Rotterdam on the city and its citizens. Video coverage of personal experiences connects to the objects on display in huge glass cases, with inspiring tales of optimism and bravery interspersed with heartbreaking stories.

While the displays' interpretative text is mainly in Dutch, translations relate the stories of the most important objects, many recovered from the rubble. Staff are also happy to help non-Dutch speakers navigate and appreciate the exhibits. Topics covered include the bombardment, the great fire that followed, the Nazis' unconscionable treatment of Rotterdam's Jewish community (and the heroic efforts by some non-Jewish locals to shelter Jewish neighbours), local resistance to the Nazi occupation and the liberation of the city by Canadian troops on 8 May 1945.

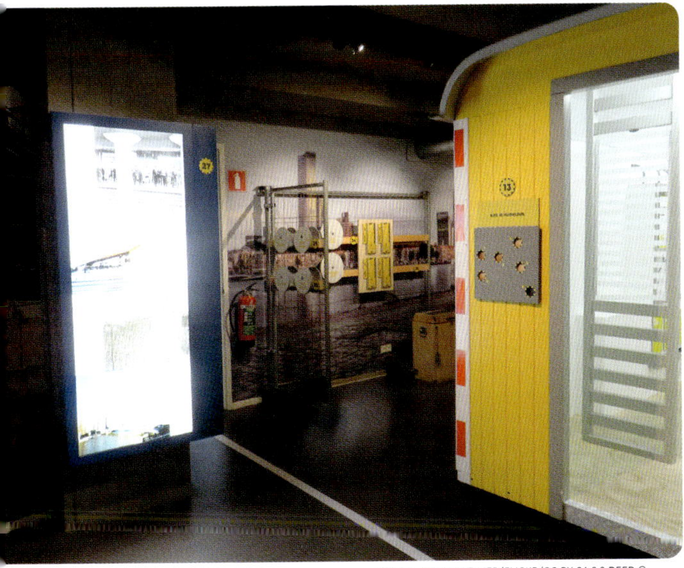

Lesser-Known Stories

The 1940 blitz wasn't the only bombing that Rotterdammers were subjected to during WWII. Displays relate how Allied air forces carried out a number of raids during the time that the Germans were in control of the city (1940–45). On 31 March 1943 one of these raids went horribly wrong, when the US Army Air Forces mistakenly bombed a residential area, killing hundreds of men, women and children. This is sometimes referred to as the 'Forgotten Bombardment'.

The Foyer

A thought-provoking and sobering display covering one wall in the foyer reminds visitors that many other cities have undergone horrific experiences such as Rotterdam's in recent times.

There's also a small but excellent selection of books on Rotterdam and WWII for sale here.

QUICK BREAK

Peaceful Het Park, east of the museum, has great places for lunch or a drink, including Parqiet and De Ballentent, both with indoor and outdoor seating.

Walk West: Delfshaven

Charming Delfshaven was one of the few neighbourhoods in Rotterdam to escape the bombs during WWII. The historic port area retains many classic attributes, including a windmill, churches and *bruin cafés* (traditional Dutch pubs), and has a slower pace of life than many other neighbourhoods. This walk takes you along its picturesque streets and waterways.

START	END	LENGTH
Oude of Pelgrimvaderskerk (metro Delfshaven)	Dudok (tram 8 Euromast)	2.6km; 2 hours

1 Pilgrim Fathers Church

Start your Delfshaven journey where the Pilgrims prayed for safe passage before departing the Netherlands aboard the *Speedwell* on 1 August 1620, changing to the *Mayflower* in Southampton and sailing to America. The **Oude of Pelgrimvaderskerk** dates from 1417 but was extensively rebuilt in the late 16th century. Church services take place at 10am and 5pm Sunday; it's usually open for visitors from noon to 4pm Friday and Saturday.

2 Windmill Tour

Walk south along Aelbrechtskolk to traditional Dutch windmill **Korenmolen de Distilleerketel**. Built in 1727 to grind corn and malt for local distilleries, it was restored in 1986 after fires in 1899 and 1940. From Tuesday to Sunday (March to October) and Wednesday, Saturday and Sunday (November to February), you can see inside (€4) and climb to the deck under the wooden sails for views across Delfshaven.

3 Power Station

Cross the VOCbrug and head east to the Lloydkwartier. An architectural masterpiece, **Schiecentrale** was Rotterdam's first power station, built in 1904. Redeveloped from 1996 to 2008 by Mei Architects, it's now home to residential apartments, commercial businesses and film studios.

4 Historic Locks

Northeast on Westzeedijk, you'll see the **Parksluizen**: a lock system constructed between 1931 and 1933 to connect the Delfshavense Schie to the Nieuwe Maas, which forms part of Schieland's main flood defence.

5 Norwegian Sailors' Church

Continue east along Westzeedijk to Het Park's northwestern edge. Built in 1914 for Norwegian mariners working at the port, and moved 170m on rolling logs in 1937 ahead of the Maastunnel's construction, the wooden **Sjømannskirken** is a treasure, with stained glass windows featuring nautical scenes and model ships suspended from the painted wooden ceiling (opening hours vary). A small shop inside sells Norwegian products including Tomtegløgg mulled wine.

6 Dutch Apple Pie

Wind your way south through Het Park, crossing the Nottebohmbrug footbridge to **Dudok in Het Park**. In a 1750 national monument overlooking an ornamental garden, it serves the city's best cinnamon-spiced *appeltaart* (apple pie).

EXPERIENCES

Ascend the Euromast (& Abseil Down)

OBSERVATION TOWER

MAP: 1 P71 **D5**

Designed by HA Maaskant to mark the Floriade 1960 horticultural expo, the 185m-high **Euromast** (*euro mast.nl; viewing platforms adult/ child from €12.50/9, with Euroscoop from €18.50/15*) offers unparalleled 360-degree views of Rotterdam from its 100m-high observation deck or its rotating 360-degree Euroscoop glass elevator; the latter goes right to the top of the mast. If you're game, the Euroscoop's glass floor offers dizzying views beneath your feet (if you're not, you can make it opaque). Download the Magnicity app to identify landmarks and explore the city through AR (augmented reality). Views are especially magical at sunset as lights illuminate the city.

You can also enjoy brunch, lunch, high tea, high wine or dinner at its panoramic restaurant (or drinks at its pop-up summer rooftop bar), or even stay overnight in two hotel suites on the observation deck, with access after dark (*from €425 including breakfast*). Thrill seekers can sign up to abseil off the tower (*€64.50, May to September/October*). Book online for the best deals.

Marvel at Rotterdam in Miniature

MODEL RAILWAY

MAP: 2 P71 **C1**

A five-minute walk west of Rotterdam's striking Centraal Station, you can see it replicated in miniature at **Miniworld Rotterdam** (*mini worldrotterdam.com; adult/child €14.70/10.50*), open Wednesday to Sunday (daily during local school holidays). Over a huge 650 sq metres, its indoor 1:87 (HO)-scale model railroad re-creates contemporary Rotterdam, with day and night simulation every 24 minutes, creating a magical effect as dusk falls and the lights switch on across the city. Fantastically intricate details include a miniature version of the city's container-filled port in operation, landmarks such as the Blaakse Bos cube houses, the Erasmusbrug, Euromast, Hotel New York and *SS Rotterdam*, and the windmill- and polder-filled countryside, with an additional section re-creating Great Britain (complete with a white chalk horse figure on the hillside). Kids will be enchanted.

Book ahead for behind-the-scenes tours of the Netherlands section (*45 minutes; €7*), which show you the model workshop and traffic control hub; there are also tours of the Great Britain section (*30 minutes; €4.70*) or both (*75 minutes; €9.40*).

Ramble in Rotterdam's Green Spaces

PARK, GARDENS

Laid out in English-garden style by father-and-son landscape architects Jan David and Louis Paul Zocher in 1852, **Het Park** (MAP: 3 P71 **D5**; *'the Park'; hetparkinrotterdam.nl*) is the city's oldest. Its 21 hectares of leafy trees, lawns, ponds and winding paths are beloved by locals, who come here to run, cycle, kick footballs around, picnic, barbecue (there's a dedicated area in the north-eastern corner), and hang out at cafes like Parqiet (p75), with deckchair seating on the grass, and **Dudok in Het Park** (MAP: 4 P71 D4), which on Sunday morning hosts intimate classical, jazz and Latin music performances (*adult/child €10/7.50; buy tickets online*).

On the eastern side of Kievitslaan (entered from Kievitslaan 8), 1.2-hectare garden **Historische Tuin Schoonoord** (MAP: 5 P71 D4; *tuinschoonoord.nl*), a former country estate, dates from the 1860s. Beyond its wrought-iron gates, its collection of 1000-or-so plant species includes giant Lebanon cedars and brown beech trees; there are also beehives, kingfishers, a tawny owl and a tranquil pond filled with Japanese carp. It's open from 8.30am to 4.30pm. Admission is free.

TENT, REPITCHED

Contemporary art platform **TENT**, (MAP: 6 P71 C4) a catalyst for eye-opening and engaging work by local creators, moved out of Centrum's Kunstinstituut Melly and is reopening in 2025 in a renovated former laboratory at Coolhaven 32 in West. Check tentrotterdam.nl for progress updates and exhibitions, performances and events in its new space.

Play Pinball in a 19th-century Grain Warehouse

MUSEUM, ARCADE

MAP: 7 P71 A4

Possibly the coolest museum in the entire country, the **Dutch Pinball Museum** (*dutchpinballmuseum.com; 2hr ticket €16, weekday/weekend day pass €27.50/30*) has scores of pinball machines: electromechanical (to 1977), solid state (to 1990) and dot-matrix (from 1991); the earliest date from the 1930s and the most recent are still being made today. It's fascinating to check out the evolution of these fantastic contraptions and cultural moments (eg 1978's banana-flippers Disco Fever, 1979's Kiss, 1984's Space Shuttle, 1992's Addams Family, 1999's South Park and Star Wars Episode I, 2015's Game of Thrones...). Better yet, you can play around 100 machines from 1960 on (admission includes games; no coins required).

The museum is set in Delfshaven's Dubbelde Palmboom, an 1825 grain warehouse that became a distillery and then a crate factory before it was abandoned; the museum relocated here from Katendrecht in 2020. It opens Wednesday, Saturday and Sunday; buy tickets ahead online as capacity is limited.

Visit a Floating Farm Shop FARM

MAP: 8 P70 C4

Where else but Rotterdam can you buy yoghurt, raw milk, butter and cheese matured below a **Floating Farm** (*floatingfarm.nl*)? On a platform on the Merwehaven, between Delfshaven and Schiedam, this revolutionary 2019-opened farm accommodates up to 40 cows, which access a harbourside pasture and produce up to 800 litres of milk each day. A second platform for poultry is in the works. Farm tours are currently for groups (check for updates), but from Tuesday to Saturday you can visit its farm shop.

Discover Distilleries & Windmills in Schiedam MUSEUMS

An aromatic 18th-century *jenever* (Dutch gin) distillery is the setting for the **Nationaal Jenevermuseum Schiedam** (MAP: 9 P70 C2; *jenevermuseum.nl; adult/child €12.50/7.50, branderij only €5/free*). Along with *jenever*-making exhibits, you'll see the distillery's huge bins, cooling vessels and copper distilling kettles, and watch stokers at work in the *branderij*, where barley and rye are still malted. A tasting of three *jenevers* costs €10.

It's worth getting a combined ticket (*€15/10*) with Schiedam's **Korenmolen de Walvisch** (MAP: 10 P70 A3; *Mill of the Whale; €8.50/5*), built in 1794 to grind malt for *jenever* production and reconstructed after a 1996 fire. Climb up inside to learn about the milling process. Its ground-floor shop sells flours milled in Schiedam.

Both museums are closed on Monday. From mid-April to October they also have combination tickets with whisper-boat cruises past Schiedam's towering windmills.

The private **Borrelmuseum** (MAP: 11 P70 D2; *tspul.nl; admission free*), open Wednesday to Sunday, has *jenever* memorabilia including posters, photographs and films. Its attached **Café-Jeneverie 't Spul** (see 11 P70 D2) stocks an incredible 500 *jenevers* and 60 gins (you can arrange guided tastings).

DUTCH DISTILLERS DISTRICT, SCHIEDAM

Infused with history (Schiedam turns 750 in 2025), this municipality on the Schie became an 18th-century hub for the production of *jenever* (traditional Dutch gin). At the industry's height, Schiedam had more than 30 windmills and 392 businesses distilling malt wine and adding juniper to produce the liquor, which was shipped all over the world. Schiedam is still home to seven central windmills (the world's tallest) and around a dozen active distilleries. They're listed on sdam.nl, along with *jenever* public artworks including a 50m fire-iron-branded, clay-tiled walkway and vintage advertising murals on and around Hoogstraat, plus festivals, gin-making workshops and guided district tours.

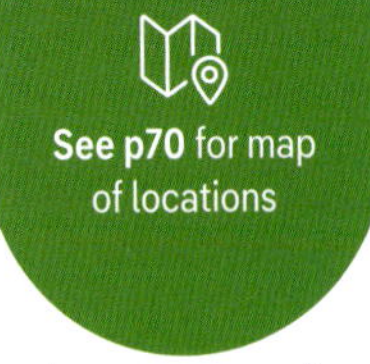

Best Places for...

€ Budget €€ Midrange €€€ Top End

Eating

Dutch

Café Steijn €€

12 P71 B3

Erwtensoep (pea soup), *rookworst* (smoked sausage) with *rode bieten* (beetroot), and *balkenbrij* (meatloaf) are specialities; in summer, dine on the terrace overlooking the Heemraadssingel canal. *11am-10pm*

't Eethuisje van Delfshaven €€

13 P71 A4

Rustic Delfshaven restaurant with grandmother-style recipes and a daily menu written on the blackboard; expect dishes like *karbonade* (pork cutlets) with *stamppot* (mashed veggies). *4-9pm Sun-Fri*

Pannenkoe Schiedam €€

14 P70 B3

Sweet and savoury Dutch *pannenkoeken* (pancakes) with gluten- and lactose-free options are available at this waterfront restaurant. Unlimited pancakes on Tuesdays. *11am-8.30pm Tue-Sun*

Contemporary

Restaurant Frits €€

15 P71 A4

Pretty Delfshaven canal house serving an astounding-value five-course surprise menu using ingredients from its own kitchen garden. It accommodates dietary requirements with notice. *6-11pm Thu-Sun*

Restaurant Goud €€€

16 P71 C5

Brass tables, golden lamps, green-velvet chairs, a recycled-champagne-bottle circular bar and multicourse menus with dishes such as shellfish *frikandel* (sausage) with wasabi crumble. *noon-3pm & 6-10pm Wed-Sat, noon-5pm Sun*

Cafes

Lilith €

17 P71 D3

Neighbourhood favourite for its all-day breakfasts including eggs (Benedict, scrambled, Florentine etc) and vegan treats such as mushrooms or avocado on toast, and plenty of gluten-free choices. *9am-5pm*

Arzu €

18 P71 C2

Maple-drizzled French toast, red-velvet pancakes and spinach-, feta- and pine nut–topped bruschetta-style croissants served all day, plus fresh mint tea, fresh-squeezed juices and cinnamon-dusted smoothies. *9am-5pm*

Vegan

Happy Food & Health €

19 P71 C3

Organic plant-based restaurant that's entirely gluten free (including the beers), with a stylish, greenery-filled dining room. *noon-9pm Sun & Tue-Thu, to 10pm Fri & Sat*

Backstage Vegan Kitchen €€

20 P71 D2

Vegan street-food dishes include seitan *rendang*, chickpea samosas, and mushroom and quinoa sliders. *noon-9.30pm Sun, Wed & Thu, to 10.30pm Fri & Sat*

Kula €€

21 P71 C4

Breakfast (cashew-milk blueberry pancakes; coconut chia pudding) and lunch (kimchi toasties; sticky tempeh bowls) in a bright space with daily yoga classes. *8am-4pm Mon-Thu, to 6pm Fri-Sun*

Drinking

Coffee

Schot Coffee Roasters

22 P71 A5

Inside the 1929 cubist expressionist Diepeveen warehouse, Schot roasts organic beans three times a week and serves them in batch-brew and hand-brew styles. *9am-5pm Wed-Sat, 10am-5pm Sun*

Evermore

23 P71 B4

Single-origin, fair trade, Rainforest Alliance beans are roasted on Wednesday and served alongside organic loose-leaf teas opposite the Coolhaven. *10am-1pm Wed-Fri, to 4pm Sat & Sun*

Urban Espresso Bar

24 P71 C3

Beans from Rotterdam roastery Giraffe are brewed by expert baristas; it also serves homemade lemonade, iced teas, organic soft drinks and Rotterdam-produced beers. *8.30am-6pm Mon-Sat, 10am-6pm Sun*

Breweries

Stadsbrouwerij De Pelgrim

25 P71 A4

Vintage brewery with bubbling copper vats and heady hops; enjoy beers such as the popular Mayflower Tripel in the bar, canal-side terrace or courtyard. *noon-midnight Wed-Sat, to 10pm Sun*

Stadshaven Brouwerij

26 P70 E4

Brews include Sailors Lager, Navigators Bock and Octopus Blond (with blood orange and kiwi-fruit). Hour-long English tours (€11.50) run at 12.30pm Saturday. *3-10pm Wed & Thu, noon-midnight Fri & Sat, noon-9pm Sun*

Eurobrewers

27 P70 B3

Glass-making warehouse-turned-brewery with a 2000-sq-metre terrace, 12 taps and locally produced *jenevers*. *4pm-2am Fri, 2pm-2am Sat, 2-10pm Sun*

Bars & Pubs

De Oude Sluis

28 P71 A4

The canal view from the terrace tables stretches to Delfshaven's windmill at this *bruin café*, which has been a popular neighbourhood spot since 1912. *noon-1am Sun-Thu, to 2am Fri & Sat*

De Machinist

29 P71 C4

Sociable bar-restaurant; the terrace overlooking Coolhaven is a great spot for a *jenever*, homemade seltzer or natural wine. *11.30am-10pm Sun-Thu, to midnight Fri & Sat*

De Kunstfabriek Unit 699

30 P71 D1

In the Groot Handelsgebouw building's gallery, a hidden passage leads to this speakeasy-style natural-wine bar serving Portuguese wines. *5pm-midnight Thu, to 2am Fri & Sat*

Live Music

Rotown

see 20 P71 D2

Popular bar and live-rock venue; the musical programme features new local talent, established international acts and crossover experiments. *noon-2am Sun, Wed & Thu, to 4am Fri & Sat*

Dizzy

31 P71 C3

Live acts perform most nights at this decades-old jazz cafe, and can include anything from cool jazz to blues-tinged sets, funk and Latin. The whisky collection is renowned. *4pm-1am*

Oase

 P71 B5

Former shipyard with cranes and skeletal ship hulks. There's local art and live music every weekend, plus festivals, markets, film nights, raves and pop-up vegan kitchens. *4pm-midnight Fri & Sat, noon-10pm Sun*

Shopping

Design

Wolff Blitz

33 P71 D2

Super-local designs include Delft-style paisley or Van Gogh sunflower shirts, Rotterdam-map or Piet Mondrian pattern sofas, and Markthal rugs. *10am-6pm Tue-Thu, 10am-8pm Fri & Sat, noon-6pm Sun & Mon*

Susan BIJL

 P71 D3

Totes, backpacks, duffle bags and raincoats using recycled fabrics such as ripstop nylon and polyester thread created from plastic bottles since the year 2000. *noon-6pm Mon, 10am-6pm Tue-Sat*

Vintage

Daily Sneaker Steals

35 P71 B3

Vintage trainers from the 80s to the early 2000s, such as Nike Air Max, Reebok Pump, Puma Sky LX, Asics Gel-Lyte and New Balance 1500. Stock changes monthly. *noon-8pm Mon-Sat, 1-8pm Sun*

Eltjo's Vintage

 P70 E2

Schiedam shop specialising in cameras from the 1940s onwards (and old film rolls). Also stocks retro record players and stereos, lamps and other electrical appliances. *10am-5.30pm Wed-Sat*

Music

De Plaatboef

 P71 D3

Rotterdam's largest new and secondhand vinyl shop, with hundreds of titles in every genre (soul, blues, rock, honky-tonk, folk, disco, trance...). *noon-6pm Sun-Thu, 10am-9pm Fri, 10am-6pm Sat*

Nooit Gewoon

38 P70 D1

Great selection of electronica vinyl popular with DJs, ranging from acid jazz to deep house and techno, dreampunk and triphop. *10am-3pm Mon-Wed, to 5.30pm Thu-Sat*

Bier & Vinyl

39 P70 D2

Browse the titles, order a beer and sit down to listen to your tunes in the living room–like lounge area. Regular live gigs and DJ sets, too. *2-5.30pm Thu, 11am-5.30pm Fri & Sat*

Chocolate

De Bonte Koe

40 P70 D2

Creations include *jenever*-filled bonbons, Delft-blue nougats and orange-chocolate crowns. There are 20-minute factory tours with tastings at 5pm Friday (€15). A vending machine filled with its artisan chocolates is nearby on Hoogstraat. *9am-5.30pm Tue-Sat, noon-5pm Sun & Mon*

Kruik

41 P70 B3

Dutch house–shaped bonbons, *stroopwafel* (syrup-filled wafer) pralines, windmill- and bicycle-printed bars and cinnamon-flavoured *drop* (liquorice). Winter hot chocolate and summer ice cream. *9am-10pm Mon-Sat, to 6pm Sun*

See p92 for eating, drinking and shopping listings

Explore Zuid

Across the Nieuwe Maas from Centrum, old Rotterdam meets new in Zuid. Architectural legacies of its shipping heritage include the Holland-America Line's former HQ, warehouses repurposed for museums, and a post-war cruise ship terminal. Zuid is also where Rotterdam's nickname 'Manhattan on the Maas' is most obvious: the skyline is punctuated by some of the city's tallest high-rises, especially around the Wilhelminapier in Kop van Zuid (South Bank). West, in Katendrecht (De Kaap; the Cape), striking new arrivals are also being built in this formerly edgy district. Between the two, the Rijnhaven's reclaimed land and floating parks are reforming the neighbourhood.

Getting Around

Metro

Lines D and E stop at Wilhelminaplein, Rijnhaven and Maashaven.

Tram

Lines 23 and 25 cross the Erasmusbrug and stop at Wilhelminaplein, Lodewijk Pincoffsweg and Vuurplaat before continuing further south-east.

Walk

Katendrecht is easily reached from Wilhelminaplein via Kop van Zuid and the Rijnhavenbrug, or by walking west from the Rijnhaven metro station.

Ferry

There are watertaxi stops on Kop van Zuid at Holland Amerikakade (near Hotel New York) and on Katendrecht at *SS Rotterdam*, Katendrechtse Haven and Katendrechtse (at Fenix II).

Hotel New York (p90)

THE BEST

SHIP TOUR
SS Rotterdam (p90)

PHOTOGRAPHY MUSEUM
Nederlands Fotomuseum (p90)

VIEWPOINT
Tornado, FENIX (p91)

CLUB
Maassilo (p91)

BREWERY TOUR
Kaapse Brouwers (p91)

For more see
Experiences p90
Eating p92
Drinking p93
Shopping p93
Erasmusbrug
Koningshaven
Stieltjesstr
Levie Vorstkade
Spoorweghaven
Wilhelminakade
Wilhelminaplein
Laan op Zuid
Nieuwe Maas
WILHELMINAPIER
Posthumalaan
Cruise Terminal Rotterdam
Holland Amerika Kade
Otto Reuchlinweg
Wilhelminakade
Koninginnenhoofd
Hotel New York
Rijnhaven
Rijnhaven

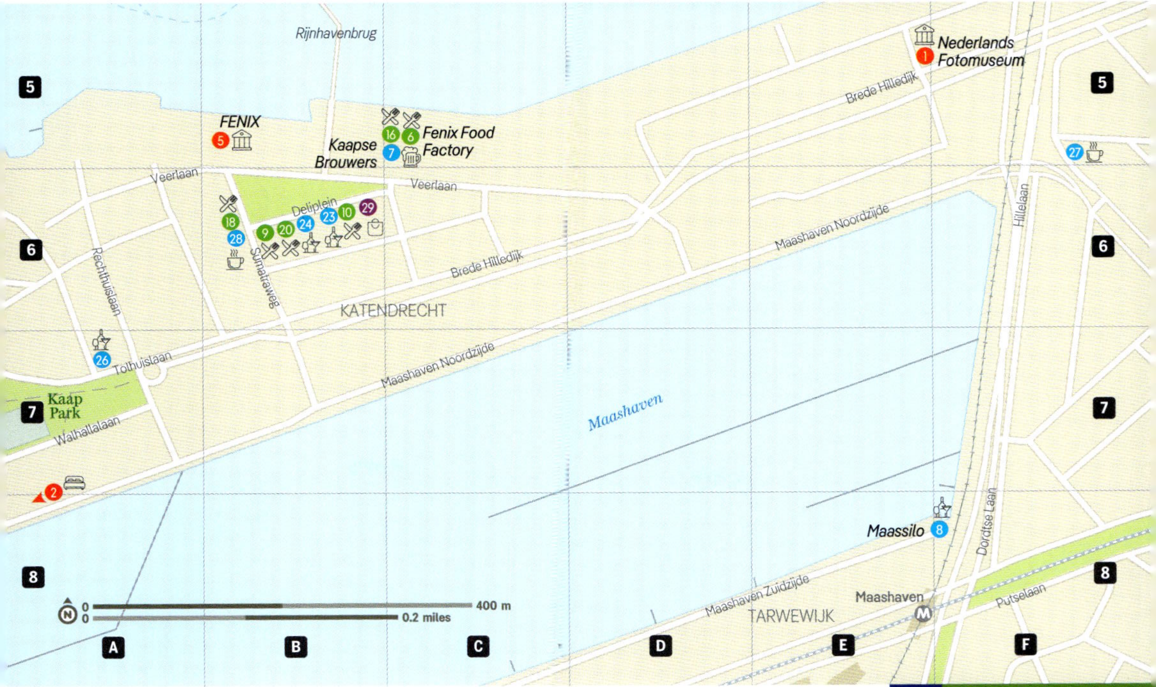
Rijnhavenbrug
FENIX
5
Kaapse Brouwers
7
16
6
Fenix Food Factory
Nederlands Fotomuseum
1
Brede Hilledijk
27
Veerlaan
Veerlaan
Deliplein
18
28
9
20
24
23
10
29
Sumatraweg
Rechthuislaan
Brede Hilledijk
Maashaven Noordzijde
Hillelaan
KATENDRECHT
26
Tolhuislaan
Maashaven Noordzijde
Kaap Park
Walhallalaan
Maashaven
2
Maassilo
8
Dordtse Laan
Maashaven Zuidzijde
Maashaven
TARWEWIJK
Putselaan
0
400 m
0
0.2 miles
A
B
C
D
E
F
5
6
7
8

Walk Zuid

Rotterdam's rapid pace of change accelerates to warp speed in Zuid. Along this route you'll see strikingly restored and repurposed shipping warehouses around Deliplein in Katendrecht, once Rotterdam's red-light district, along with dizzying new skyscrapers, and the creation of a whole new neighbourhood rising from the reclaimed Rijnhaven, with floating parks in the harbour.

START	END	LENGTH
Set Sail (metro Rijnhaven)	Erasmusbrug (metro Leuvehaven)	3.5km; 3 hours

1 Pylon Murals

Beneath the metro tracks, 18 pillars supporting the line above have been painted by Dutch and international artists and local children as part of the Rotterdam Art Ride ('ROAR'). Right outside Rijnhaven metro station is **Set Sail** (2018) by Rotterdam street artist Tymon de Laat. It depicts a skipper looking out over the Rijnhaven's former port.

2 Local Square

Katendrecht (De Kaap; 'the Cape'), once a district of brothels, opium dens and dive bars, has undergone a metamorphosis. **Deliplein**, near cultural-heritage and community centre Verhalenhuis Belvédère and opposite the redesigned Fenix warehouses, still has a long-standing tattooist and is the area's vibrant cafe and restaurant hub.

3 Lost Luggage

Cross the Rijnhavenbrug footbridge to Holland Amerikaplein, where Jeff Wall's 2001 sculpture **Lost Luggage Depot** features cast-iron suitcases, trunks and duffel bags representing the belongings of emigrants who boarded the Holland-America Line here.

4 Floating Park

A third of Rijnhaven's harbour basin is being filled in over the coming years, reclaiming land for high-rise commercial and residential developments and parkland, with floating parks accessed by footbridges and jetties. Its first **Rijnhaven Floating Park** is built from plastic debris retrieved from Rotterdam's waterways, with a buoy-marked summertime swimming area.

5 Warehouse Food Hall

The 17th-century Dutch East India Company (VOC) warehouse Pakhuismeesteren now houses a hotel, Room Mate Bruno, on its upper-level addition, and post-industrial **Foodhallen**, with 13 independent food and drink stands.

6 Hyper High-Rise

Heading to Pakhuismeesteren's northern side on the Nieuwe Maas' Wilhelminapier you'll see the soaring **De Rotterdam**, a 2013 completed 'vertical city' of three interconnected towers designed by OMA's Rem Koolhaas. It incorporates offices, apartments, the now hotel, bars and restaurants.

7 The Swan

Continue along Wilhelminakade to cross the **Erasmusbrug**, locally dubbed 'de zwaan' – a graceful, all-white cable-stayed bridge (its southernmost span has an 89m-long bascule, opening to allow taller ships to pass). Designed by architect Ben van Berkel and completed in 1996, it stretches 802m across the Maas. (In strong winds you can end your walk at Zuid's Wihelminaplein metro station.)

EXPERIENCES

See the Nederlands Fotomuseum MUSEUM

MAP: 1 P86 **E5**

The nation's premier platform for visual storytelling, the **Nederlands Fotomuseum** (*Netherlands National Museum of Photography; nederlandsfotomuseum.nl; adult/child €16/free*), closed Monday, curates diverse exhibitions from its exceptional collection of over six million images that reflect Dutch photography from 1842 on, and mounts topical temporary exhibitions.

Since 2007 it has been located on the Wilhelminapier in the Las Palmas building, once the workshops of the Holland-America Line, but at research time it was set to move into its spectacular new home, the Pakhuis Santos on the Rijnhaven in Katendrecht, in autumn 2025. Built between 1901 and 1903 to store coffee, this bluestone-based red-brick warehouse was redesigned by Rotterdam's WDJArchitecten and Hamburg's Renner Hainke Wirth Zirn Architekten, and topped with a two-storey glass-and-lacy -aluminium 'crown'. The building's eight open-plan floors will house archives, studios, a photography bookshop, a ground-floor cafe and a panoramic restaurant overlooking the city.

Board the SS Rotterdam SHIP TOUR

MAP: 2 P86 **A7**

A harbour landmark, the Holland-America Line's elegant former flagship, 'La Grande Dame' **SS Rotterdam** (*ssrotterdam.com; tours adult/child from €12.95/8*), has become a hotel moored across from its old HQ (now Hotel New York).

Tour options include the 90-minute Sea Breeze Deluxe, taking in the upper decks, bow, bridge and wheelhouse; hour-long Steam & Chrome, visiting the engine room; or 2½-hour Complete Tour. Its on-boerd restaurants, bars and terrace are also open to the public.

Among the world's largest passenger ships – 228m long, 28m wide and 51m high – when christened by Queen Juliana in 1958, the SS Rotterdam made its maiden voyage to New York the following year. After its last crossing in 1971, it became a cruise ship before being restored and returning home to Rotterdam.

Admire the Holland-America Line's Former HQ ARCHITECTURE

One of Rotterdam's most recognisable buildings, the **Hotel New York** (MAP: 3 P86 **B4**; *hotelnewyork.com*) occupies the Holland-America Line's former headquarters on the Wilhelminapier. It was built from red brick in Jugendstil (Art Nouveau) style in 1901; the second of its two copper-domed clock towers was completed in 1917. After aviation overtook transatlantic crossings, the building was sold but lay empty before the city of Rotterdam bought it in 1988, opening as a hotel in 1993.

Public spaces include its cafe-restaurant and waterside terrace, and atmospheric pre-war

Manhattan-style NY Basement (open Wednesday to Saturday); book for Frank Sinatra tribute acts.

Much of Rotterdam's Holland-America Line infrastructure was destroyed during WWII's bombings and replaced directly after the war. Among them was the Wilhelminapier's **Cruise Terminal Rotterdam** (MAP: 4 P86 **B3**), with six distinctive shell roofs and glazed side elevations. Designed by Brinkman, Van den Broek & Bakema, it was completed in 1949 and restored by Tom David Architecten in 2015.

Savour Craft Beers at Fenix I

ARCHITECTURE, TAPROOM

Katendrecht's warehouses Fenix I and Fenix II were originally a single warehouse, San Franciscoloods – the world's largest warehouse when it was built in the 1920s for the Holland-America Line. They were split during their 1950s reconstruction.

Topped in 2019 by a huge residential loft and cultural development by Mei Architects, Fenix I is home to **Fenix Food Factory** (MAP: 6 P87 **C5**; *fenixfoodfactory.nl*). An open-concept drinking and dining space (closed Monday), it has a bookshop, zero-waste kitchen, natural wine bar, soda bar and bakery, plus a terrace overlooking the Wilhelminapier. Its biggest draw is Kaapse Kaap, the tasting room of craft brewery **Kaapse Brouwers** (MAP: 7 P86 **C5**), with 20 of its own and international beers on tap and more in its shop. Book online for three-hour behind-the-scenes tours (*kaapsebrouwers.nl; €55*) in English, from Fenix to/from the Keilehaven brewery (travelling by watertaxi).

FENIX II'S NEW MIGRATION MUSEUM

Migration is the heart of 2025-opening museum **FENIX** (MAP: 5 P86 **B5**; *fenix.nl*), in Katendrecht's 1920s-built warehouse Fenix II. Stunningly renovated by MAD Architects, the 16,000-sq-metre space is topped with a double-helix stainless-steel-and-timber 'tornado' staircase accessing a 24m-high viewing platform overlooking the Holland-America Line's former HQ and quays that saw millions of voyages.

The new museum has acquired hundreds of contemporary artworks and commissioned many more. Exhibits also include photographs capturing family, departure and arrival, home sickness and happiness, and personal items such as a maze of 2000 suitcases donated from around the world. Here, too, is a 2000-sq-metre 'covered city square', Plein.

Dance in a former Grain Silo

CLUB

MAP: 8 P86 **F8**

A silo dating from 1910 is now the epic venue of **Maassilo** (*maassilo.com*), with a capacity of 4000. At 40m high, its Now&Wow Club has fab views and techno-driven beats. Event hours and ticket prices vary.

LISTINGS

Best Places for...

€ Budget €€ Midrange €€€ Top End

See p86 for map of locations

Eating

Modern Dutch

De Matroos en Het Meisje €€

 B6
With Delftware-style Katendrecht mural illustrations and a Deliplein terrace, 'The Sailor and the Girl' has three- to five-course chefs menus. *6-10pm Mon-Fri, noon-4pm & 6-10pm Sat & Sun*

NOTK €€

 B6
Sommelier-run wine bar–restaurant with house-milled sourdough accompanied by hand-churned oyster butter, and sustainable seafood and vegetable dishes. *5-11pm Wed & Thu, noon-4pm & 5-11pm Fri & Sat, 1-8pm Sun*

Views

Putaine €€

11 C4
Floating in the Rijnhaven; chef Michael Schook ferments his own vegetables and uses Delfshaven-landed seafood in dishes such as sea bass with razor-clam tartare. *5-10pm Mon, noon-4pm & 5-10pm Tue-Sat*

Restobar Vista €€

12 C2
By the water on De Rotterdam's ground floor with stunning views, and natural wines to match its organic menu. *noon-2.30pm & 5.30-9.30pm Wed-Sun*

Hotel New York Café-Restaurant €€

 B4
On the Nieuwe Maas with an oyster bar, French dishes such as asparagus and goats-cheese quiche or chateaubriand, and one of Rotterdam's best waterside terraces. *11am-11pm*

Ono €€

 B4
Modern Japanese restaurant overlooking the Rijnhaven and serving artistically presented dishes like charcoal-grilled yellowtail with wasabi ice cream. *5-10pm Tue-Sun*

International

Foodhallen Rotterdam €€

 C3
In the Pakhuismeesteren warehouse, 12 food stands encompass New York–style pizza, Javanese Indonesian, *bao* and dim sum, burgers, *bitterballen* (deep-fried, crumbed balls with ragu filling) and Vietnamese street food. *noon-10pm*

Fenix Kitchen €€

 C5
At Katendrecht's Fenix Food Factory; order a changing line-up of locally sourced international dishes such as burgers by QR code. *11am-9pm Tue-Thu, to 10pm Fri & Sat, to 8.30pm Sun*

By Ami €€

 C3
Technicolour street-art 'forest' and Rijnhaven terrace with a menu spanning Peking duck pancakes, sea bass ceviche and Black Angus sliders. *11am-10pm*

Cafes

Koffiebar Namaste €

18 B6
All-day breakfasts (eg spinach shakshuka), pastries (such as gluten-free tahini chocolate brownies), and artisan coffee from Schot Coffee Roasters. *10am-5pm Wed-Sun*

Rolph's Deli €

 C3
Bagels (eg pastrami and mustard), rolls (lobster and

truffle mayo) and open sandwiches (smashed avocado and Pata Negra); look out for upcoming evening dining. *9am-4pm Mon-Fri, to 3pm Sat*

Jordy's Bakery €

 B6

Has four locations, including this one on Deliplein; cookies, cakes, croissants, sandwiches and sourdough pizzas emerge from the stone oven. *8am-6pm*

Drinking

Cocktails

Elvy

 C2

On De Rotterdam's nhow Hotel's 7th floor, with a skyline-view terrace; cocktails include the Fat Sailor (dark rum, Kahlua and lime juice). *noon-midnight Sun-Thu, to 2am Fri & Sat*

NY Basement

22 B4

In the Hotel New York, with old-school jazz (and Sunday Sinatra concerts); cocktails include the whisky-and-Dom Benedictine Sinatra Vieux. *5pm-midnight Wed & Thu, to 1am Fri & Sat, to 11pm Sun*

Bar Break

 B6

Enjoy reinvented cocktails such as Long Island iced tea with coffee foam or a camomile-infused 'apple-tini' in the exposed-brick interior or on the Deliplein terrace. *3-11pm Sun, Wed & Thu, to 1am Fri & Sat*

Live Music

Café De Ouwehoer

 B6

Atmospheric *bruin café* (pub) on Deliplein, often with live music acts. *3pm-midnight Tue-Thu, 3pm-2am Fri, 2pm-2am Sat, 2pm-midnight Sun*

Café Dox

25 D2

Inside the Nieuwe Luxor Theater overlooking the Rijnhaven, with weekly live music (mostly acoustic singer-songwriters and bands), Rotterdam-brewed beers and natural wines. *9am-8pm Mon, to 11pm Tue-Sat*

Café Norge

 A7

Bruin café with live gigs and DJs on weekends, plus karaoke, quiz nights, a pool table, a street-side terrace and a toasty open fireplace. *2pm-1am Sun-Thu, to 2am Fri & Sat*

Coffee

Café Prêt à Boire

 F5

A cafe by day (wine bar by night) serving locally roasted beans from Shokunin Coffee and A Matter of Concrete, and great cinnamon rolls. *4-11pm Thu-Sat*

Kopi Soesoe

 B6

V60, AeroPress, filter and espresso coffees served at picnic tables on Deliplein or in the lounge room-style interior. Live acoustic music some nights. *8am-5pm Mon-Fri, 9am-6pm Sat & Sun*

Shopping

Health & Beauty

Tattoo Bob

 B6

A Katendrecht – and Rotterdam – legend, Bob has been tattooing here on De Kaap since 1968, and now also does tattoo removal and permanent makeup. *1-10pm Mon-Sat*

New York Barbershop

 B4

A traditional barbershop since 1884 in the Hotel New York, with straight razor wet shaves, moustache and beard treatments, and haircuts. *9am-6pm Tue-Fri, to 3pm Sat*

Explore South Holland

Worth a Trip

South Holland's Walking and Cycling Tours

Kinderdijk (p132)
VERVERIDIS VASILIS/SHUTTERSTOCK ©

See 107 for eating, drinking and shopping listings

Explore Delft

Enchanting Delft, an amalgam of medieval and 17th-century treasures, has one of the Netherlands' most exquisite town centres. Its narrow, canal-threaded streets, patterned-brick Markt square and picturesque churches make it appear scarcely changed since revered artist Johannes Vermeer lived and painted here, yet Delft is also a lively university city with a vibrant arts scene. Situated midway between Rotterdam (just 12 minutes away by train or 45 by bike) and Den Haag (14 minutes by train or 30 by bike), it's a popular day-trip destination, but an overnight stay allows you to experience the city at its least crowded and most magical.

Getting Around

Train

Intercity and Sprinter trains link Delft with Rotterdam (19 minutes) and Den Haag (12 minutes).

Walk

From Delft station, it's a 500m walk north-east to reach Markt in the heart of Delft.

Tram

Lines 1 and 19 run north from Delft station along Phoenixstraat to Delft's northern edge.

THE BEST

CHURCH
Nieuwe Kerk (p104)

FACTORY TOUR
Royal Delft (p105)

MARKET SQUARE
Markt (p104)

ART CENTRE Vermeer Centrum Delft (p100)

CANAL EXPLORATIONS
Sloepverhuur Delft Randstad Recreaties (p106)

Delft
CHUNYIP WONG/GETTY IMAGES ©

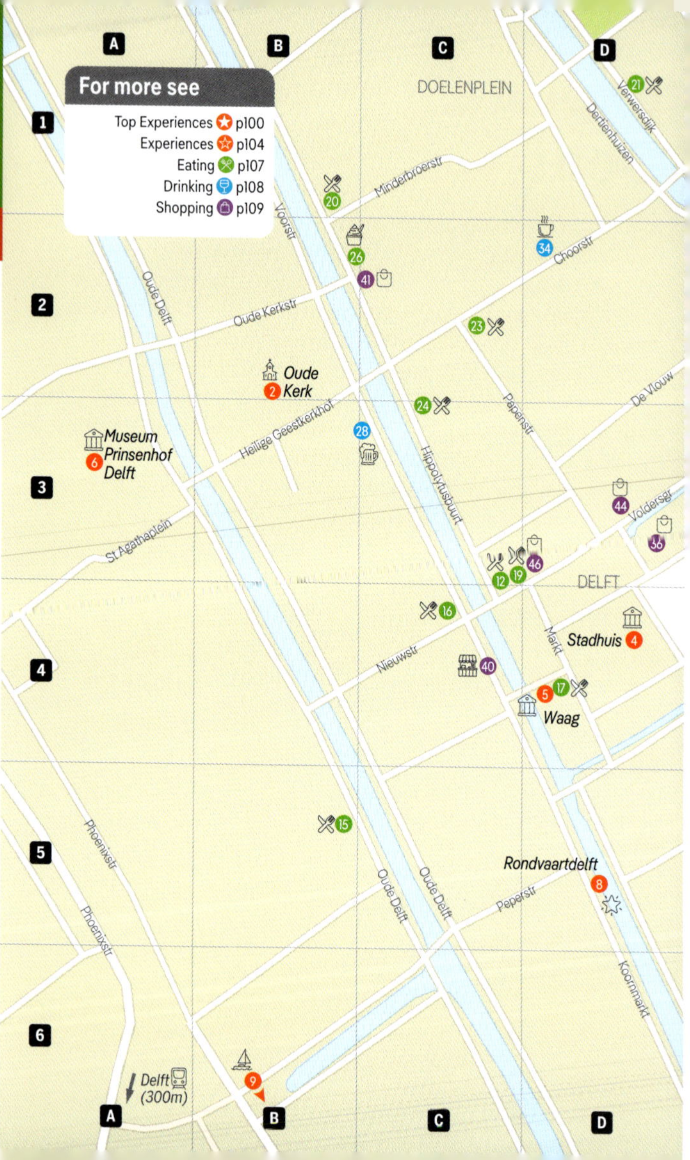

For more see

Top Experiences p100
Experiences p104
Eating p107
Drinking p108
Shopping p109

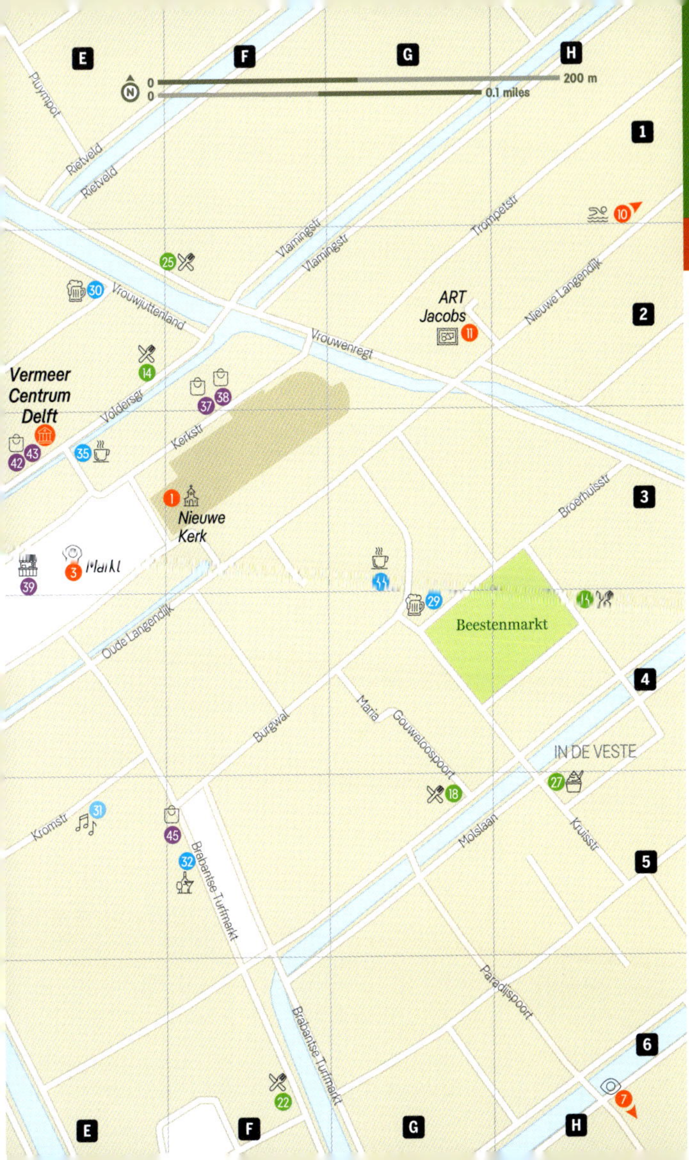

E
F
G
H
0
0
200 m
0.1 miles
1
2
3
4
5
6
Pluympot
Rietveld
Rietveld
Vlamingstr
Vlamingstr
Trompetstr
10
25
30
Vrouwjuttenland
ART Jacobs
11
Nieuwe Langendijk
Vrouwenregt
14
Vermeer Centrum Delft
Voldersgr
37
38
42
43
35
Kerkstr
1
Nieuwe Kerk
Broerhuisstr
3
39
29
Beestenmarkt
Oude Langendijk
Burgwal
Maria
Gouwelcospoort
IN DE VESTE
27
18
Kromstr
31
45
32
Brabantse Turfmarkt
Molslaan
Kruisstr
Paradijspoort
Brabantse Turfmarkt
22
7
E
F
G
H

★ TOP EXPERIENCE

Vermeer Centrum Delft

The great painter Johannes Vermeer was born in Delft in 1632 and lived here until his death in 1675. While none of his works remain in the town, this centre fills the gap with reproductions, video presentations and displays about 17th-century painting techniques and materials.

MAP P98 **E3**

PLANNING TIP
Cubes throughout Delft's historic centre mark significant places for Vermeer, the centre sells a booklet (*€3; English available*) for the Vermeer cube walk, illustrating the artist's life in the city.

Downstairs

In a reconstructed building on the historic site of the former St Lucas Guild, where Vermeer was Dean of Painters for four years, the information centre **Vermeer Centrum Delft** (*adult/child €12/6*) is a great place to learn about the artist.

Start by watching the short video presentation about Vermeer's life (multiple languages available through audiophones) before wandering past 37 actual-size, high-quality digital reproductions of his paintings. Viewing them all together gives a comprehensive overview of Vermeer's complete body of work. The replicas are arranged in chronological order, allowing you to appreciate the development of Vermeer's subjects and techniques throughout his career. Detailed information also makes viewing a great primer for seeing some of Vermeer's originals at the **Mauritshuis** (p114) in Den Haag and the Rijksmuseum in Amsterdam.

Upstairs

Afterwards, head upstairs (the building is fully wheelchair accessible) to the centre's most interesting exhibits – a display on the pigments and tools that Vermeer would have used during his all-too-short working life and an interactive display on how he used light and shadow in his work. He is called 'the master of light' for good reason.

You'll also learn about the restoration in 2010 of Vermeer's *Woman in Blue Reading a Letter*

Scan for practical information.

(1663–64), part of the collection of the Rijksmuseum in Amsterdam. The painstaking restoration was funded with revenue gained by sending the painting to feature in various exhibitions in galleries around the world. During the intricate process, yellow varnish covering the work was removed and the Rijksmuseum's conservators were able to ascertain how Vermeer produced such an intense blue colour: he used a copper-green undercoat to give his blue extra depth.

Temporary Exhibitions & Events

The centre also presents temporary Vermeer-related exhibitions, such as works by local artists, still-life flower photography or recycled clothing made from Vermeer city marketing banners, and occasionally hosts hands-on activities. The gift shop has a superb range of items, from napkins and tableware to reproductions on canvas.

QUICK BREAK
Vermeer may well have visited **De Waag** (p105) when it functioned as a weigh house; now you can visit this landmark to enjoy a drink, light lunch or upmarket dinner.

Walk Delft

Vermeer's hometown might not have any of his original paintings on display, but Delft isn't lacking in art. This walk takes you past visually arresting public artworks by local artists, celebrating the city's heritage in everything from old maps of the historic canal-threaded centre to street-art murals and sculptures inspired by Delft's iconic blue-painted porcelain.

START	END	LENGTH
Delft Station	Beesenmarkt	1.5km; 2 hours

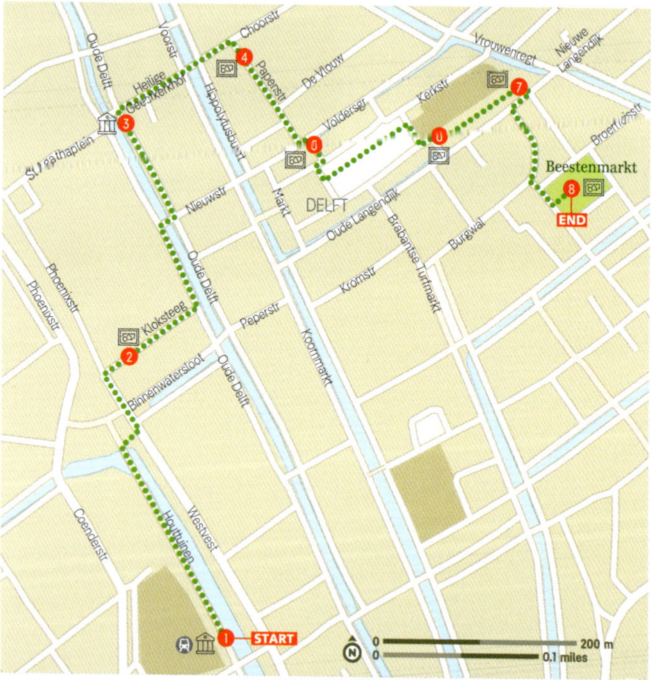

1 Cartographic Art

At Delft's light-filled **railway station**, designed by Delft-founded architectural firm Mecanoo and opened in 2015, look up to see its curved aluminium ceiling featuring a stylised 1877 map of Delft's canals. The station's hall, walls and columns feature contemporary impressions of Delft blue tiles.

2 Street Art

Head north along Westsingelgracht to Kloksteeg's 2019 mural **De Gouden Eeuw** (The Golden Age) by Micha de Bie; at the western end it depicts famous Delft figures including Hugo de Groot and Vermeer's girl with a pearl earring. Further along, building facades are painted in colours in Pieter de Hooch's 17th-century paintings. Scan the QR code on the wall for details.

3 Phone-box Gallery

Follow the Oude Delft canal north, crossing 17th-century footbridge Jeronymusbrug to **Voor de Kunst**, a phone booth converted by Tijn Noordenbos in 1973 that serves as a micro gallery space for Delft artists.

4 Mosaic Mural

Pass the Oude Kerk and cross the Nieuwe Delft canal to reach the **Keramieken Kaart van Delft** (2020) by Nan Deardorff McClain, a 17th-century map of Delft in mosaic tiles with hidden stories, symbols and quirky facts.

5 Delftware Laneway

Walk south on Papenstraat to Voldersgracht; narrow laneway **Bonte Ossteeg** (Colourful Ox) has two delftware tributes, a stencilled electrical box topped by a blue-and-white ox sculpture, and a Delft-blue mural covering an entire wall. Both were created by Hugo Kaagman in 2013.

6 The Blue Heart

Cross Markt towards the Nieuwe Kerk's southern side, where Marcel Smink's striking 1998 steel-and-blue-glass sculpture **Het Blauwe Hart** is illuminated from within at night.

7 Milkmaid Sculpture

On the Nieuwe Kerk's northern side, Wim T Schippers' **Het Melkmeisje** is a tribute to Vermeer's 1658 painting. Created in concrete and stucco, it was installed in 1976 to commemorate the 300th anniversary of Vermeer's death.

8 Colourful Cow

Walk south on Burgwal to Beestenmarkt. At the centre of what was once the town's cattle market is Rob Brandt's 1993 red, yellow and blue glazed-pottery **Koe** (Cow); today the square is lined by restaurants and cafes.

EXPERIENCES

Climb the Tower of Delft's Nieuwe Kerk

CHURCH

MAP: 1 P98 F3

Gracing Delft's skyline with the Netherlands' second-highest tower (after Utrecht's Domtoren), the **Nieuwe Kerk** (*oudeenniewuwekerkdelft.nl; adult/child with Oude Kerk €8.50/4*) is only 'new' in relation to the city's Oude Kerk (Old Church). After an apparition here in 1351 recurred for the next three decades, construction began in 1381 on a temporary wooden church, with the basilica built around it from 1384; it was completed in 1655.

The Nieuwe Kerk has been the final resting place of almost every member of the House of Orange since 1584, including William of Orange (Willem the Silent), who lies in an over-the-top marble mausoleum designed by Hendrick de Keyser. Statesman Hugo de Groot is also buried here. Other interior highlights include its 1839-built organ with over 3000 pipes; kerkconcertendelft.nl has concert programmes.

Climbing 376 narrow, spiralling steps in its 109m-high tower (*€6/3.50, with Nieuwe and Oude Kerks €13/5*) rewards with views to Rotterdam and Den Haag on a clear day (*kids must be over six*).

Pay Homage to Vermeer at the Oude Kerk

CHURCH

MAP: 2 P98 B2

Willem II granted Delft city rights in 1246, the church's official founding date, though it actually dates from an earlier wooden church here in 1240. Originally known as Sint Bartholomeusas, its 75m-high, 1350-completed tower leans nearly 2m from the vertical due to subsidence caused by its canal location, giving it its nickname Scheve Jan ('Leaning John'). Halfway up in its oak belfry, one of its two bells rings every half-hour.

From 1396 the church was known as Sint Hippolytuskerk until the Nieuwe Kerk's construction, when it became the **Oude Kerk** (*oudeennieuwekerkdelft.nl; adult/child with Nieuwe Kerk €8.50/4*). Its older section features an austere barrel vault; the newer, early-16th century northern transept has a Gothic vaulted ceiling. Its beautiful carved main pulpit dates from 1548, surviving fires and Reformation ransacking. Its 2832-pipe organ is played during services and concerts (*kerkconcertendelft.nl*).

Look for Johannes Vermeer's memorial stone, upgraded in 2007, the 300th anniversary of the painter's death, and the grand black-and-white-marble tomb of naval hero Piet Hein.

Visit Delft's Monumental Markt

MARKET, ARCHITECTURE

One of the largest historic market squares in Europe, the rectangular **Markt** (MAP: 3 P98 E3) has had a market here since the 13th century and was first paved in the late 15th century. The Nieuwekerk looms over its north-eastern end, with the **Stadhuis** (MAP: 4 P98 **D4**), Delft's town hall, at the south-eastern end, its Renaissance construction surrounding an early-14th-century tower. Behind it, the **Waag** (MAP: 5 P98 **D4**; p107), Delft's 16th-century weighing house, remained in use until 1960. It now houses the cafe-restaurant De Waag.

Markets still set up here on Thursday, with around 150 stalls selling fresh fruit, vegetables, cheeses, spices, flowers, homewares, as well as plenty of blue-and-white Delft souvenirs.

See How Delftware Pottery is Made at Royal Delft

FACTORY

MAP: 7 P98 **H6**

In the 17th century Delft had 32 factories producing Delft blue earthenware, but today only one remains. Koninklijke Porceleyne Fles, trading as **Royal Delft** (*museum.royaldelft.com; adult/child €15/7*), 1.5km south of the Markt, has been handcrafting its blue-and-white-painted porcelain since 1653.

Allow around an hour for an audio-guide tour of its museum, where pieces include William III's personal collection, which he donated to the company in 1887, and polychrome Royal Delft has produced since 1879. The tours also lead you through a painting demonstration and the factory's production process, ending in the gift shop.

Book ahead to attend a workshop (*from €37.50*), held at 2pm Tuesday to Sunday, where you can paint your own piece of Delft blue (tiles, plates etc). There are also workshops specifically for children.

For a real treat, reserve ahead for high tea (*€27.50, minimum two people*), served on Delft blue tableware at its Brasserie1653 (it also serves lunch). Delft Blue Line tickets include a canal cruise (*from €23.25/10*).

RENOVATING THE MUSEUM PRINSENHOF DELFT

MAP: 6 P98 **A3**

The convent where William of Orange (Willem the Silent) was assassinated in 1584 – he was the world's first political leader to be murdered with a handgun; the bullet hole in the wall is preserved – now houses the **Museum Prinsenhof Delft** (*museum prinsenhofdelft.nl*). At research time it was set to close in early 2025 for renovations to add a lift (for accessibility) and create a new entrance to allow natural light to stream through the building. There'll also be a cafe, a shop and a hands-on studio, and exhibitions centred on William the Silent, the Delft masters and delftware. It reopens in spring 2027.

Cruise Delft's Canals

BOATING, WATER SPORTS

Delft is especially picturesque viewed from its waterways. From April to October, **Rondvaartdelft** (MAP: 8 P98 **D5**; *rondvaartdelft.nl; adult/child €12.50/5.50*) has cruises departing hourly between 11am and 5pm from Koornmarkt 113, with multilingual commentary on the city's landmarks and its history.

To explore the waterways under your own steam, from April to September you can rent a boat with **Sloepverhuur Delft Randstad Recreaties** (MAP: 9 P98 **B6**; *randstadrecreaties.nl*), based at Westsingelgracht, next to Delft's train station. Its eco-friendly whisper boats accommodate up to six adults; instruction and route maps are provided (no boat licence required), with life jacket rental available. Prices for two-/four-hour blocks start at €89/159; there are also great add-ons such as *cava* (and glasses), *borrel* (snack) platters, lunch boxes and even high-tea boxes.

For an even closer view, **Sup & Surf Delft** (MAP: 10 P98 **H1**; *supdelft.nl*) runs guided three- to four-hour SUP tours (*€27.50*), taking you under bridges and past beautiful cityscapes, stopping at a waterside cafe en route. If you don't have experience, it runs 75-minute beginner SUP lessons (*€20*). Check dates online beforehand.

Watch a Delft Artist at Work

ART

MAP: 11 P98 **G2**

If Delft artist René Jacobs is in his Nieuwe Langendijk studio-gallery **ART Jacobs** (*artjacobs.nl*) when you visit, you're welcome to watch him at work. Otherwise, you can check out his creations, which have included more than 100 pieces with original perspectives on the paintings of Delft's most famous artist, Johannes Vermeer. You can buy works in the gallery. It's always open on Friday and Saturday, and often Monday to Thursday (check ahead).

VERMEER'S DELFT

The great Dutch Master Johannes Vermeer (1632–75) lived his entire life in Delft, fathering 15 children, 11 of whom survived infancy, and leaving behind fewer than 40 paintings. (The actual number is disputed, as the authorship of some canvasses attributed to him has been questioned by modern-day Vermeer experts.) Vermeer's subjects were drawn from everyday life in Delft, his interiors depicting domestic scenes and his portraits remarkably lifelike. Vermeer's best-known exterior work, *View of Delft* (c 1660–61) captures the light and shadow of a partly cloudy day. It's possible to visit the location where he painted it, across the canal at Hooikade, south-east of the train station.

See p98 for map of locations

Best Places for...

€ Budget €€ Midrange €€€ Top End

Eating

Dutch

De Visbanken €

 12 C3

Fish has been sold on this spot since 1342. Display cases in the old open-air pavilion entice with fresh, marinated, smoked and fried fishy treats. *9am-6pm Tue-Fri, to 5pm Sat*

Spijshuis de Dis €€

13 H4

Old-fashioned gem with outdoor tables on the Beestenmarkt and dishes including fish soup served in a bread roll, beer-braised rabbit stew, and gingerbread cake soaked in cinnamon liqueur. *5-10pm Tue-Sat*

Cafes

Kek €

 14 E2

Fronted by baskets of organic fruit and vegetables used in fresh smoothies and juices, and dishes such as loaded waffles, yoghurt trifles and brunch tacos, with Rotterdam-roasted Giraffe coffee. *8.30am-4.30pm Wed-Mon*

Stads-Koffyhuis €€

 15 B5

Famous for its lunchtime sandwiches such as aged Gouda and fig jam on rye bread or smoked salmon, spinach and pesto on white poppyseed farmers rolls. *9am-5pm Mon-Sat, 11am-4pm Sun*

Bombina €€

 16 C4

Corner cafe overlooking Wijnhaven popular for breakfast and brunch, with choices such as eggs royale on English muffins or pancakes with bacon and maple syrup. *8.30am-5pm Tue-Sun*

Historic Settings

De Waag €€

 17 D4

In the 16th-century weigh house on Markt, with a sprawling terrace perfect for a post-sightseeing beer and a hearty, meat-dominated menu. *11am-9pm Mon-Wed, Fri & Sat, 10am-9pm Thu, 11am-6pm Sun*

Stadsherberg de Mol €€

 18 G5

Built in 1465, with half-metre-thick brick walls and hefty oak beams, Burgundian menus and weekend medieval banquets (clothing rental €5). *6-10pm Wed, Thu, Sat & Sun, 7-11pm Fri*

De Centrale €€€

 19 C3

The 16th-century grain and meat storehouse De Koornbeurs now has sustainably focused four-to seven-course surprise chef's menus with natural-wine pairings. *6-10pm Sun-Thu, 5.30-10pm Fri & Sat*

Italian

Il Tartufo €

 20 B1

Aromatic deli stocking Italian wines, takeaway breads, pastas and cured meats, and in-house cafe with red-and-white chequered tablecloths for on-site dining. *noon-8pm Mon, 11am-8pm Tue-Fri, 10am-5pm Sat*

La Fontanella €€

D1

The ultimate Italian neighbourhood restaurant, La Fontanella has been at this location since 1974 and has a floating summer terrace. It imports its ingredients from Italy. *5-10pm Tue-Sun*

San Marco €€

F6

On the Brabantse Turfmarkt, with wood-fired pizzas, fresh pastas and traditional meat and fish mains; save room for desserts such as chocolate ricotta cannelloni or pistachio tiramisu. *5-10pm*

Bakeries

Stadsbakkerij de Diamanten Ring €

C2

Baking since 1799; must-tries include its Delftse Bol (choux pastry filled with whipped cream and topped with chocolate) and Delft's best *appeltaarten* (apple pies). *8am-6pm Mon-Sat, 9am-5pm Sun*

Bakker Suikebuik €

C3

Cookies are the speciality here: baked meringue, chocolate-dipped *bokkepootjes*, shortbread-style *roomboter spritsen*, and spiced, almond-covered *janhagel*. It also serves high tea. *8am-5pm Tue-Sat, noon-5pm Sun*

Les Gâteaux €

F2

French patisserie specialising in quiches; its 40 varieties include goat cheese, walnut and honey; wild mushroom and truffle; and Lorraine. *11am-6pm Wed-Fri, 10am-5pm Sat*

Ice Cream

Chocolaterie De Lelie €

26 B2

Organic milk and yoghurt from the nearby Groene Hart *polder* (drained land) area, and fruit from 1838-founded greengrocer Koos Bertels are used in sublime ice creams. *10am-10pm Mon-Sat*

IJs & Zo €

H5

Over 80 ice creams and sorbets in flavours such as caramelised pistachio, pepper and vanilla, *jenever* melon, and sea buckthorn; gluten-free cones available. *1-9pm Wed-Sun*

Drinking

Beer

Delfts Brouwhuis

28 C3

Delft's youngest brewery (2019) brews five beers that are gravity fed to taps in its bar below, plus Dutch craft beers. *11am-1am Sun-Thu, to 2am Fri & Sat*

Café-Brasserie Belvédère

29 G4

Belgian beer is the popular choice here (there are 15 on tap), enjoyed at a sea of tables in leafy Beestenmarkt. *noon-1am Sun & Mon, 11am-1am Tue-Sat*

Doerak

30 E2

Canal-side and pavement seating, a long indoor bar and a huge array of craft and Trappist beers, 12 of which are on tap. *2pm-1am Mon-Thu, to 2am Fri, noon-2am Sat, 1pm-1am Sun*

Bebop Jazzcafé

E5

Jam sessions on Tuesday, concerts every Wednesday, 90 beers and a large whisky collection. *7pm-midnight Mon, 4pm-1am Tue-Thu, 3pm-2am Fri, 2pm-2am Sat*

Locus Publicus

F5

Cosy local favourite with 200-plus beers, including 15 on tap; tastings available (€12 for four accompanied by a bar snack). *4pm-1am Tue-Thu, to 2am Fri & Sat*

Coffee & Tea

Cortado Cafe

G3

Serving house-speciality *cortado* (espresso with a drop of milk), cappuccino and iced coffee brewed from Amsterdam's Lot 61 beans, and teas such as mint and jasmine. *9am-5pm*

Neef Rob

 D2

Coffee served 20 ways, including spiked with its own coffee liqueur, amaretto or whisky, and more than 100 loose-leaf tea varieties, plus artisanal chocolates. *10am-5pm Tue-Sat, noon-5pm Sun*

Tazz

35 E3

Loose-leaf teas and dirty chai, plus coffees like espresso, iced pour-overs and pumpkin-spiced lattes using Delft-roasted Miss Morrison beans; spiked milkshakes and smoothies too. *10am-5pm Thu-Tue*

Shopping

Delftware

Royal Delft Brandstore

36 D3

Official outlet on the Markt of Delft's only remaining porcelain factory, Royal Delft; certificates of authenticity supplied with each piece. *9.30am-6pm Mon-Sat, 10am-6pm Sun*

De Blauwe Tulp

 F2

Delftware is painted and sold in this studio and shop near the Markt. *10am-5pm Mon-Sat Mar-Sep, shorter hours Oct-Feb*

De Candelaer

38 F2

Delftware outfit De Candelaer is located just off the Markt; you can watch its artists at work. *9.30am-5pm Mon-Fri, 10am-5pm Sat*

Markets

De Markt

 E3

Farmers and flower market dating back to the 12th century; held on the Markt square with more stalls along Brabantse Turfmarkt. *9am-5pm Thu*

Antiekmarkt

 C4

Over 100 stalls spread along Hippolytusbuurt, Voorstraat and Wijnhaven selling tableware, delftware, Dutch antiques, books, art and more. *10am-4pm Sat mid-Apr–Sep*

Art & Design

Voorlopig

41 C2

Stocks a monthly changing selection of ceramics, art, bags, jewellery, clothing and children's books made by over 70 local artists. *10am-6pm*

Pleck

 E3

Colourful clothes and homewares fills this shop, which also has a cafe section with courtyard seating. *10am-5.30pm Tue-Thu, 10am-6pm Fri & Sat, noon-5pm Sun*

Droom

43 E3

Candles, vases, picnic ware, wallets and perfumes by Dutch designers are among the items displayed on the shelves here. *noon-5.30pm Mon-Fri, 11am-5.30pm Sat, noon-5pm Sun*

Music

Plexus

 D3

Thousands of titles in mint or near-mint condition, including rare recordings by Led Zeppelin and the Miles Davis Quintet. *noon-6pm Mon, 10am-6pm Tue-Thu & Sat, 10am-9pm Fri, noon-5pm Sun*

Sounds

 F5

Informed staff have good suggestions at this 1999-opened shop selling new and secondhand vinyl. *noon-6pm Mon, 9.30am-6pm Tue-Fri, 9.30am-5pm Sat, noon-5pm Sun*

Velvet Music

 D3

Vinyl, CDs, cassettes and DVDs in genres ranging from reggae and world music to jazz to traditional Dutch ballads. *noon-6pm Mon, 9.30am-6pm Tue-Sat, noon-5pm Sun*

See p127
for eating,
drinking and
shopping
listings

Explore Den Haag

Stately Den Haag (The Hague; locally known as 's-Gravenhage, 'The Counts' Hedge') is the Dutch royal residence and seat of government (though Amsterdam is the country's capital), and home to the under-renovation Binnenhof parliament on the Hofvijver lake, and institutions including the UN at the Vredespaleis (Peace Palace). Its regal buildings contain sublime galleries, museums and theatres, but the Netherlands' third-largest city also has statement-making new architecture and vibrant drinking and dining scenes, especially around the Grote Kerk in the centre and out near the fishing harbour at the southern end of the long, golden-sand beach at Scheveningen.

Getting Around

Train

Intercity and Sprinter trains link Den Haag Centraal Station with Rotterdam Centraal Station (30 minutes) via Delft (12 minutes).

Tram

Line 1 links Den Haag with Rotterdam (25 minutes). Lines 15 and 17 traverse Den Haag's centre. Lines 1, 9 and 11 run to Scheveningen.

Walk

From Den Haag Central Station it's a 1km walk west to the city centre.

Vredespaleis (p125)

ANKOR LIGHT/SHUTTERSTOCK ©

THE BEST

ART GALLERY
Mauritshuis (p114)

SURFING
Scheveningen (p123)

CHURCH TOWER
De Haagse Toren, Grote Kerk (p122)

CULTURAL COMPLEX
Amare (p125)

MEDIEVAL PRISON
Rijksmuseum de Gevangenpoort (p122)

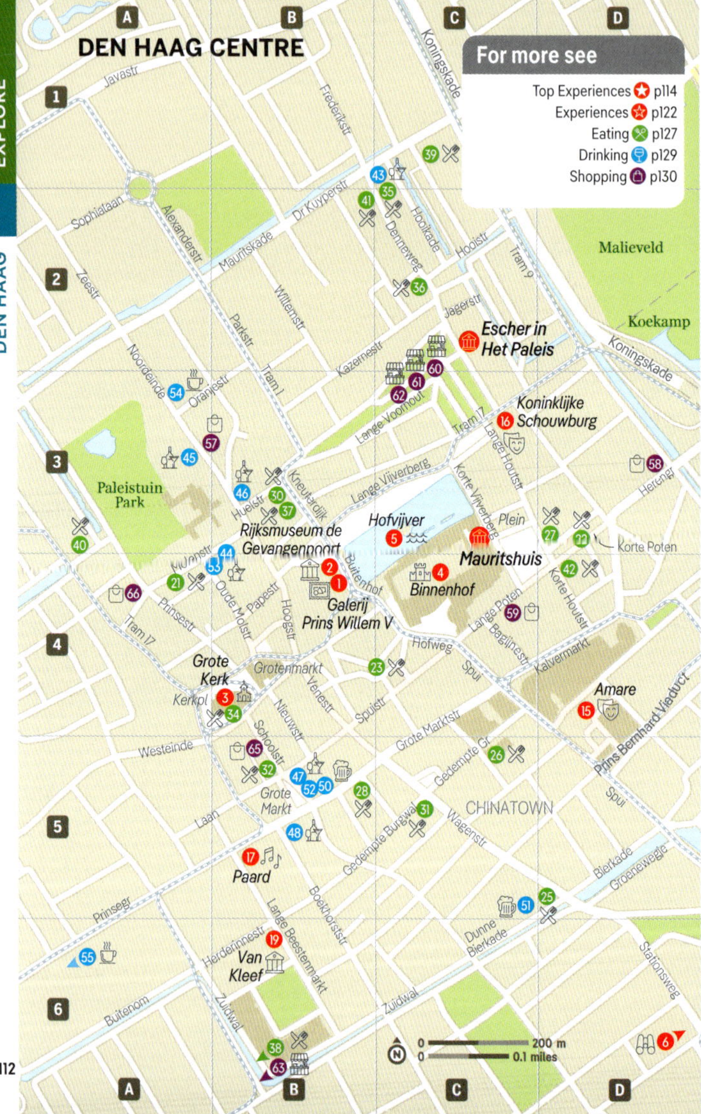
DEN HAAG CENTRE
For more see
Top Experiences p114
Experiences p122
Eating p127
Drinking p129
Shopping p130
Escher in Het Paleis
Koninklijke Schouwburg
Hofvijver
Mauritshuis
Binnenhof
Rijksmuseum de Gevangenpoort
Galerij Prins Willem V
Grote Kerk
Paard
Van Kleef
Amare
CHINATOWN
Paleistuin Park
Malieveld
Koekamp
Grote Markt
200 m
0.1 miles

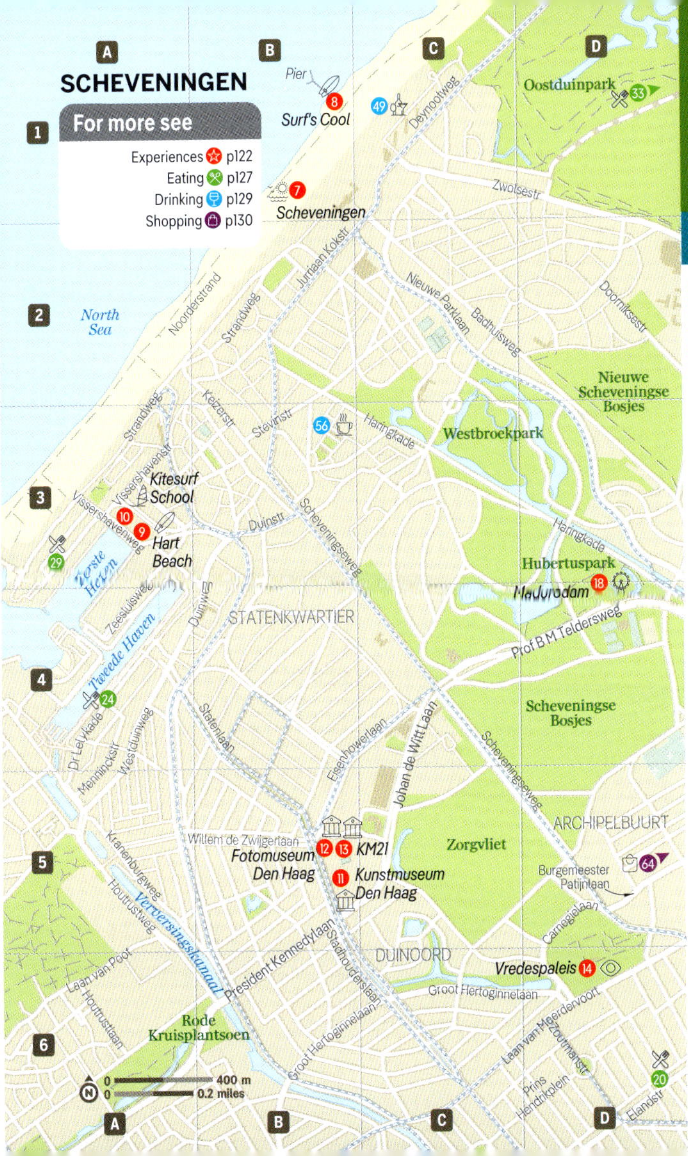
SCHEVENINGEN
For more see
Experiences p122
Eating p127
Drinking p129
Shopping p130
A
B
C
D
1
2
3
4
5
6
North Sea
Pier
8
Surf's Cool
49
7
Scheveningen
Oostduinpark
33
Deynootweg
Zwolsestr
Jurriaan Kokstr
Noorderstrand
Strandweg
Nieuwe Parklaan
Badhuisweg
Doornikseestr
Nieuwe Scheveningse Bosjes
Westbroekpark
Keizerstr
Stevinstr
56
Haringkade
Strandweg
Vissershavenstr
Kitesurf School
Vissershavenweg
10
9
Hart Beach
29
Eerste Haven
Duinstr
Scheveningseweg
Haringkade
Hubertuspark
Madurodam
18
Zeesluisweg
Duinweg
STATENKWARTIER
Prof B M Teldersweg
Tweede Haven
24
Dr Lelykade
Statenlaan
Eisenhowerlaan
Johan de Wittlaan
Scheveningse Bosjes
Scheveningseweg
Menninckstr
Westduinweg
ARCHIPELBUURT
Willem de Zwijgerlaan
12
13
KM21
Fotomuseum Den Haag
Zorgvliet
Kranenburgweg
11
Kunstmuseum Den Haag
Burgemeester Patijnlaan
64
Houtrustweg
Verversingskanaal
Carnegielaan
President Kennedylaan
Stadhoudersaan
DUINOORD
Laan van Poot
Vredespaleis
14
Groot Hertoginnelaan
Houtrustlaan
Laan van Meerdervoort
Zoutmanstr
Rode Kruisplantsoen
Groot Hertoginnelaan
Prins Hendrikplein
20
Elandstr
0 400 m
0 0.2 miles

★ TOP EXPERIENCE

Mauritshuis

One of the world's great art museums, the Mauritshuis is the repository of masterpieces from the Dutch golden age of painting. The collection features works by a who's who of the 17th-century Dutch and Flemish art worlds – Vermeer, Rembrandt, Rubens, Hals and many others are well represented.

MAP P112 **C3**

PLANNING TIP
To avoid missing out, prepurchase your ticket online to secure your time slot (the museum is quietest after 3pm). Download the free multimedia smart tour app from app stores.

Scan this QR code for opening hours and other information.

The Museum

Spectacularly situated on the reflective Hofvijver, adjacent to the Binnenhof, the Mauritshuis (*adult/child €19.50/free*) has housed the Royal Cabinet of Paintings since 1822. It was privatised in 1995 and expanded in 2014, unveiled by King Willem-Alexander. Its predecessor, the **Galerij Prins Willem V** (p122), can be visited on the same ticket.

Jewels of the Collection

One of the museum's most recognisable works is *Ice Scene* (c 1610), in Room 16, by Amsterdam-born artist Hendrick Avercamp, depicting skaters on a frozen river with windmills and thatched houses in the background. Carel Fabritius' lifelike *The Goldfinch* (1654), in Room 14, is another exquisite masterpiece worth seeing.

The collection is rich in portraits. These include Rembrandt's huge, gruesome *The Anatomy Lesson of Dr Nicolaes Tulp* (1632), painted in Amsterdam when the artist was only 25, in Room 9. More Rembrandts can be found in the next room. Look out too for Hals' lovely portraits of Aletta Hanemans (1625) and her husband Jacob Olycan (1625) in Room 10.

Standing above all others for its charm and fame, Vermeer's *Girl with a Pearl Earring* (c 1665) is the pride of the museum's collection. It hangs in Room 15, alongside Vermeer's *View of Delft* (c 1660–61) with its wonderful interplay of light and shade.

LEX VAN LIESHOUT/ANP/AFP VIA GETTY IMAGES ©

Re-examining the Past

The Mauritshuis occupies the 1641-built mansion designed in Dutch classicism style by architect Jacob van Campen for Count Johan Maurits van Nassau-Siegen (1604–1679), governor of the colony of Dutch Brazil, captured from the Portuguese by the Dutch West India Company (WIC) for its sugarcane plantations and mills. In recent years the museum has addressed Maurits' role in the transatlantic trade in enslaved people between west and central Africa and Brazil. A permanent exhibition in Room 8 features works such as *Brazilian Landscape with a House under Construction* (c 1655–60) by Frans Post, who was among the artists and scientists who travelled with Maurits to Brazil. The exhibition, along with the museum's ongoing research, aims to encourage debate.

QUICK BREAK

The museum's Brasserie Mauritshuis serves contemporary lunch dishes made from local ingredients inspired by the museum's paintings and is an elegant place for an afternoon beer or glass of wine.

★ TOP EXPERIENCE

Escher in Het Paleis

Celebrating Dutch graphic artist MC Escher (1898–1972), this museum in the 18th-century Lange Voorhout Palace displays more than 120 of Escher's woodcuts and lithographs, including many of his best-known works. Fascinated by mathematical patterns, Escher investigated themes of repetition, circularity, infinity and symmetry throughout his career.

MAP P112 **C2**

PLANNING TIP
Escher in Het Paleis is closed on Monday. Tickets are sold on its website. Money-saving combination tickets with the Mauritshuis or the Panorama Mesdag are available online from Tiqets (*tiqets.com*).

Scan this QR code for full opening hours and ticket prices.

Lange Voorhout Palace

Constructed between 1760 and 1764, the building was designed by Pieter de Swart for Anthony Patras, mayor of Sloten and the States General representative. Later owned by the Hope family, financers of European nobility (Napoleon stayed briefly in 1811), it was purchased in 1896 by Queen Emma (great-great grandmother of current king Willem-Alexander), who used it as a winter residence until her death in 1934.

The museum (*adult/child €12.50/0.50*) moved into the building in 2002, perhaps attracted by its beautiful staircase, which appears to go up to the 2nd floor but doesn't, a very Escher-like optical illusion.

Other striking features within the building are the parquet floors by American minimal art practitioner Donald Judd (1928–94) and dramatic chandeliers designed by Dutch sculptor Hans van Bentem (b 1965).

Escher's Early Works

MC (Maurits Cornelis) Escher's early works feature woodcuts, many inspired by his trips to Italy. In 2024 the museum acquired one of his earliest woodcuts, a counterproof White Cat that Escher made in 1919 when he moved to Haarlem to study at the School of Architecture and Decorative Arts and was given a pet white cat by his landlady. It's dedicated to his nephew Rudolf. When the museum removed the mount it revealed Escher's handwritten text about the print that had been concealed.

DUTCH CITIES/ALAMY STOCK PHOTO ©

Among the museum's highlights is the dizzyingly precipitous *Tower of Babel* (1928), a well-known example of Escher's early experimentation with perspective.

The Metamorphoses

A circular work inspired by Escher's preoccupation with the interlinked concepts of eternity and infinity, *Metamorphosis III* (1967–68) evokes time and space running parallel in an unending circle. His largest-ever print, the 7m-long work was printed on 33 blocks on six combined sheets before being partly coloured by hand and mounted on canvas. Its imagery includes an Italian city, a chess game, bees, fish, birds, horses and boats. Two other *Metamorphosis* works (I and II) show a similar preoccupation with the theme of the cycle.

QUICK BREAK
Queen Emma's former kitchen, with beautiful floor and wall tiling, now houses the MC Café, a lovely spot for tea, coffee, juices and cakes – check ahead to reserve high tea.

WALKING TOUR

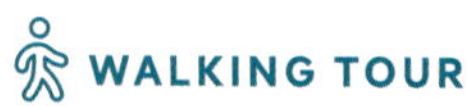

Walk Den Haag: Historic Centre

Den Haag's grandeur shines on this walk past its most important buildings. Starting outside one of its royal palaces, survey the progress of renovations to the Dutch parliament's historic Binnenhof complex from atop a viewing platform. Next, admire the city's ceremonial former town hall and mightiest church before ending at the palace gardens.

START	END	LENGTH
Paleis Noordeinde (tram 1 Kneuterdijk)	Paleistuin (tram 17 Torenstraat)	1.3km; 2 hours

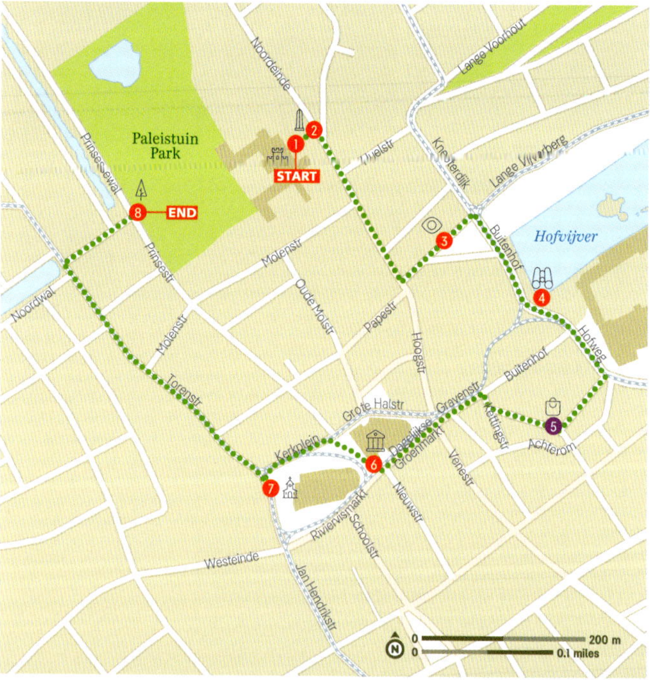

1 Royal Workplace

King Willem-Alexander's official offices are at **Paleis Noordeinde** (he and his family live at Huis ten Bosch, north-east of Den Haag's city centre). Originally a medieval farmhouse, it was enlarged by Frederik Hendrik, Prince of Orange, Count of Nassau, between 1640 and 1645, creating its current 'H' form. It's open on select days each summer; check koninklijke verzamelingen.nl.

2 Regal Statue

Across the street from the palace gates, the **Ruiterstandbeeld Prins Willem van Oranje** (Equestrian Statue of William of Orange), by Emile de Nieuwerkercke, dates from 1845.

3 Renovation Centre

Head south-east along Noordeinde to Plaats, the former forecourt of the Binnenhof, now a public square. The **Informatiecentrum Binnenhof Renovatie** (*binnenhof renovatie.nl*) has details of the Binnenhof's multiyear renovation (p123) and archaeological finds unearthed during the process.

4 Viewing Platform

A short walk east by the reflective Hofvijver lake, the **Kijksteiger Uitzichtpunt** is a 28m-high viewing platform overlooking the Binnenhof's renovation works. Climb its 149 steps to see the mirrored construction shed, which has a coastal dune roof garden to blend it into its surrounds.

5 Historic Arcade

South-east, just off Hofweg, enter **De Passage**, an 1885-built, glass-roofed shopping arcade (the Netherlands' oldest) with a 2014 extension. Shops range from high-end fashion to specialist chocolate and coffee boutiques.

6 Old City Hall

Walk south-west on Gravenstraat to the Groenmarkt. **Het Oude Stadhuis**, built in 1664–65 and extended in 1733, is a splendid example of Dutch Renaissance architecture, with stepped gables, pediments, brick and natural stone. Dutch royal births are registered here; the building is otherwise now mainly used for weddings.

7 Great Church

Opposite on the Groenmarkt is Den Haag's magnificent **Grote Kerk**, still the site of royal weddings and baptisms (both Willem-Alexander and his daughter Catharina-Amalia, Princess of Orange, were baptised here).

8 Palace Gardens

Head north-west to Veenkade to enter the **Paleistuin**. Laid out in the 17th century, the Noordeinde's palace gardens, open sunrise to sunset, have hedgerows, flowerbeds, fountains, ponds, and tree-flanked lawns for picnics.

Walk Den Haag: City to Seaside

An extraordinary cylindrical painting of Scheveningen – the oldest 19th-century panorama still displayed in its purpose-built original location – is the ideal place to begin this walk to the coast it depicts, via avenues, forest and rose gardens. It's easy to return to central Den Haag by tram; alternatively, this entire route is perfect for cycling.

START	END	LENGTH
Panorama Mesdag (tram 1 Mauritskade)	De Pier (tram 1/9 Kurhaus)	5.5km; 2½ hours

1 Panoramic Painting

Start at the **Panorama Mesdag** (*panorama-mesdag.nl; adult/child €16/12*), closed Monday. This immense, 14m-high, 360-degree painting of the sea, dunes and fishing village of Scheveningen, 120m in circumference, was created in 1881 by Hendrik Willem Mesdag of the Impressionist-influenced Hague School of painters. From an upper platform it gives the illusion you're high on a dune looking at the scene.

2 Woodland Walk

Head north-west along Zeestraat and then Scheveningseweg. Past the Peace Palace, a bronze bust of poet Constantijn Huygens, who proposed this tree-lined thoroughfare, marks the entrance to the forested, squirrel-filled **Scheveningse Bosjes**, a dune area planted with oaks, elms and poplars in the 17th century, with snowdrops, foxgloves, and wild hyacinths in spring.

3 Rose Garden

Exiting the Scheveningse Bosjes on the northern side at the Cremerbrug, you'll pass the 1953 monument to Social Democratic Workers Party leader Pieter Jelles Troelstra (1860–1930), where Labour Day is commemorated on 1 May. Take the footbridge to the 1920s-created, English-style **Westbroekpark**. From June to November, 20,000 roses in 300 varieties bloom in its rosarium. Sculptures include the charming bronze *De Gelaarsde Kat* (Puss in Boots; c 1943) by Den Haag artist Johan Keller (1863–1944).

4 Seafarers' Church

Kapelweg leads to Scheveningen. Appearing in the Panorama Mesdag, the former fishing village's oldest remaining building is the **Oude Kerk Scheveningen** (*oudekerkscheveningen.nl*), dating from 1466. Its ceiling represents an upturned ship's hull; look too for the stained-glass window featuring a ship with red sails, and a 17th-century whale jawbone.

5 Fishing Heritage

Follow Keizerstraat to the beachside promenade, where Gerard Bakker's poignant 1982 bronze sculpture the **Vissersvrouw van Scheveningen** (Fisherman's Wife) stares out to sea. Footsteps north, Marcel van Zijp's 2013 granite-and-concrete Vissersnamenmonument records the names of 1366 fishermen who have drowned offshore.

6 Pleasure Pier

North-east along the seafront, **De Pier** (*pier.nl*), Scheveningen's 382m-long pier, built in 1961 to replace the 1901 pier destroyed in WWII, has a Ferris wheel, a bungy jump, a zipline, an arcade including pinball machines, and copious eateries.

EXPERIENCES

Visit the Netherlands' First Museum GALLERY

MAP: 1 P112 B4

The **Galerij Prins Willem V** (*mauritshuis.nl; adult/child €5.50/free*) was the first public museum in the Netherlands when it opened in 1774 as a showcase for William V's art collection. It closed after many of its works were 'acquired' by the occupying French in 1794 and didn't reopen in the same location until 2010.

Today the fully restored gallery, adorned with silk and chandeliers, displays over 150 old masters from the Mauritshuis collection (by Bloemaert, Potter, Rubens, Steen et al) hung cheek-by-jowl in the style of the late 18th century. If you're visiting the jewel in Den Haag's artistic crown, the **Mauritshuis** (p114), tickets include entry here; otherwise you can buy tickets on arrival (no time slots required).

Dare to Enter a Medieval Prison MUSEUM

MAP: 2 P112 B4

A remnant of the 13th-century city fortifications, the Gevangenpoort functioned as a prison from 1428 to 1825. Now the **Rijksmuseum de Gevangenpoort** (*gevangenpoort.nl; adult/child €15/7.50*), it evokes the experiences of both prisoners and their jailers.

You can explore the chilling building with a free audioguide, or book in for a 45-minute guided tour (*extra €5; tours in English run at 1pm Saturday and Sunday*), with guides bringing medieval crime and punishment vividly to life. There are special interactive audioguides for older children, but the museum's displays (branding irons, flogging benches and frightening torture devices) mean it's not suitable for kids aged under eight.

On weekends and holiday periods especially, it's best to book time-slot tickets ahead online. The museum adjoins the **Galerij Prins Willem V** (the two institutions share an entrance).

Climb the Grote Kerk's 600-year-old Tower CHURCH, TOWER

MAP: 3 P112 B4

Den Haag's landmark **Grote of Sint-Jacobskerk** (*Great Church or St James' Church; grote-kerk.nl; adult/child €3/free*) is one of the city's oldest buildings. A wooden chapel was built in 1256, and construction of the stone church began in 1335. The building expanded to its current size during the 15th century, and the carved wooden pulpit was added in the 16th century. Its hexagonal tower, **De Haagse Toren**, was completed in 1424; the city carillonneur plays its 80m-high, 51-bell carillon from noon to 1pm on Monday, Wednesday and Friday. Other than Dutch royal occasions, the church no longer holds services. Its opens to visitors noon to 4pm Thursday to Sunday March to October and noon to 4pm Saturday and Sunday November to February (buy tickets on arrival), and hosts concerts, organ recitals and art exhibitions (check the agenda online).

Climbing the tower's 288 steps provides spectacular city views. Prebook hour-long tower tours (*dehaagsetoren.nl; €8.50/6.50*), held in English at 1pm Thursday to Sunday in summer and 1pm Saturday and Sunday the rest of the year.

View a New York-Inspired Skyscraper

ARCHITECTURE

MAP: 6 P112 **D6**

Not to be confused with the Grote Kerk's six-century-old church tower De Haagse Toren, award-winning skyscraper **Haagse Toren** (*haagsetoren.nl*) on Rijswijkseplein was completed in 2007. Visible across the city, it's nicknamed Het Strijkijzer (The Iron); its architect Paul Bontenbal was inspired by New York's 1902 Flatiron Building.

The 132m-high tower contains offices and apartments. Its 42nd-floor 'city balcony' observation platform and 'sky bar' currently only open for business events; check online for updates.

RENOVATING THE BINNENHOF

In autumn 2021 work began on renovating one of the world's oldest parliaments and the country's oldest monumental structure. Home to both houses of the Dutch parliament, the 4000-room, 90,000-sq-metre **Binnenhof** (MAP: 4 P112 **C4**; Inner Court) by the **Hofvijver** (MAP: 5 P112 **C3**) ranges around a central courtyard once used for executions; its ceremonial Ridderzaal (Knights Hall) dates from the 13th century. The buildings' condition was worse than foreseen, and spiralling costs and heightened security requirements (including a fortified bunker for logistics operations) have so far quadrupled the budget to €2 billion and delayed completion until the end of 2028. Parliament meanwhile meets in a temporary building on Bezuidenhoutseweg.

Hit the Waves at Scheveningen

WATER SPORTS

Seaside **Scheveningen** (MAP: 7 P113 **B1**) is a favourite escape for its 4.5km-long golden-sand beach averaging 110m wide, with plenty of water sports.

On the pier, **Surf's Cool** (MAP: 8 P113 **B1**; *surfscool.nl*) runs two-hour surf lessons for adults (*€39.50*) and kids (*€25*), and 1½-hour SUP lessons (*€35*).

If you're already proficient, **Hart Beach** (MAP: 9 P113 **A3**; *hartbeach.nl*) rents boards (*per hour from €10*), as well as SUPs, skinboards (and skateboards), plus wetsuits, gloves, hoods and booties.

At Scheveningen's harbour Vissershavenweg, **Kitesurf School** (MAP: 10 P113 **A3**; *kitesurfschool.nl*) has 3½-hour beginner courses (*€110*) to multiday courses (*from €389*).

Discover De Stijl at the Kunstmuseum Den Haag

MUSEUM, GALLERIES

A 1935 geometric Art Deco masterpiece designed by HP Berlage houses the **Kunstmuseum Den Haag** (MAP: 11 P113 **B5**; *kunstmuseum.nl; adult/child €19/free*), showcasing fine arts, applied arts and fashion. Its flagship permanent exhibition Mondrian & De Stijl displays the world's largest collection of Piet Mondrian paintings, including his unfinished Victory Boogie Woogie (1942–44). Other permanent exhibitions are Discover the Modern, featuring Austrian artist Egon Schiele's beautiful *Portrait of Edith* (1915) among early-20th-century works by artists such as Van Gogh, Kandinsky, Monet and Picasso; and Delftware WonderWare, with an extensive collection of Delftware pottery. Temporary exhibitions are excellent. Kids aged nine and up love the interactive Wonderkamers ('wonder rooms') and there are activities for younger children, too. The museum closes on Monday.

The adjacent **Schamhart Wing**, built in 1962 and named for its architect Sjoerd Schamhart, contains both the photography museum **Fotomuseum Den Haag** (MAP: 12 P113 **B5**; *fotomuseumdenhaag.nl*) and contemporary art museum **KM21** (MAP: 13 P113 **B5**; *km21.nl*). Tickets are €14/free. The wing is also closed on Monday. (Even though it's affiliated with the neighbouring Kunstmuseum, there are no combination tickets available.)

THE DUTCH ROYALS

A constitutional monarchy since 1814, the Kingdom of the Netherlands' ruling House of Orange-Nassau (*royal-house.nl*) has roots in the 16th century when Spain's Philip II appointed William of Orange (William the Silent) as stadtholder (governor and commander-in-chief). Dutch royals have no substantive power within the government, performing a largely ceremonial role. After living in exile in WWII, Queen Wilhelmina abdicated for her daughter, Queen Juliana, who abdicated in 1980 for her daughter Queen Beatrix; her own abdication in 2013 ended more than a century of female reign when her son Willem-Alexander acceded the throne with his wife, Máxima. The eldest of their three daughters, Catharina-Amalia, is heir apparent.

Tour the Peace Palace

NOTABLE BUILDING

MAP: 14 P113 **D6**

The UN's Permanent Court of Arbitration and International Court of Justice, the **Vredespaleis** (*Peace Palace; vredespaleis.nl*) occupies a grand building donated by American steelmaker Andrew Carnegie; the first stone was laid in 1907, and it opened in 1913. Its free visitor centre (*open Wednesday to Sunday*) has 30-minute audio tours detailing the history of the building and the organisations here.

Book up to two weeks ahead online for hour-long guided tours. 'Inside the Palace' tours (*€16.50*) visit the art-filled Great Hall of Justice, Small Hall of Justice and Japanese room. 'Outside the Palace' tours (*€12.50*) take in the grounds and historic garden, where sculptures include Hildo Krop's 1913 bronze-and-stone statue of Erasmus pointing to the Grand Courtroom.

You'll need a passport (or EU identity card/driving licence), and you must store your belongings (including phones/cameras) in lockers during tours.

Outside the gates, the 2002-installed Wereldvredesvlam (World Peace Flame) is surrounded by stones from UN countries, including fragments from the Berlin Wall, and Robben Island, where Nelson Mandela was imprisoned.

Catch a Live Performance

LIVE PERFORMANCE

Cultural hub **Amare** (MAP: 15 P112 **D4**; *amare.nl*) is a vast 54,000-sq-metre complex designed by Patrick Fransen (of NOAHH) and Jo Coenen (JCAU) and unveiled in 2021. Behind its 'theatre curtain' facade its 1500-seat concert hall, 1300-seat 'danstheater', 600-seat ensemble hall and 200-seat rehearsal hall are home to the Nederlands Dans Theater (Netherlands Dance Theatre; NDT), Koninklijk Conservatorium (Royal Conservatory) and Residentie Orkest (Philharmonic Orchestra). Public spaces host free events. Early September's Spotlight Festival launches the year's cultural calendar.

A theatre since 1804, the beautiful [illegible]-seat **Koninklijke Schouwburg** (Royal Theatre; MAP: 16 P112 **C3**) was built in 1766 by Pieter de Swart in Louis XVI style as a palace for Prince Karel Christiaan van Nassau-Weilburg (brother-in-law of Stadtholder William V). The programme of Het Nationale Theater (The National Theatre; hnt.nl) includes English-language and other performances that don't require knowledge of Dutch.

Den Haag's biggest, most electrifying and eclectic venue for rock, pop, jazz, folk, Afro beats and more, including club events and parties, is **Paard** (MAP: 17 P112 **B5**; *paard.nl*), with 1100- and 300-capacity stages and a 200-capacity cafe space.

Walk Around a Miniaturised Netherlands

AMUSEMENT PARK

MAP: 18 P113 D4

On the edge of the Scheveningse Bosjes woodland, the delightful **Madurodam** (*madurodam.nl; admission from €22.50*) has 1:25-scale versions of a mini Netherlands, containing Schiphol, Amsterdam, windmills and tulips, Rotterdam's harbour, train stations, the Delta dykes and more. The level of detail and lifelike moving parts such as taxiing planes and sailing ships are astonishing.

Walking around the miniature 'country' takes about an hour. Kids love hands-on exhibits that include generating wind-powered energy, building dykes and managing Dutch ports, and playgrounds including an indoor one themed around the Dutch masters. On-site restaurants include the Panorama Café, overlooking the park. Tickets are cheaper online, or you can buy them on arrival.

Sip Jenever in a Historic Distillery

MUSEUM

MAP: 19 P112 B6

Once a production hub for *jenever* (traditional Dutch gin), Den Haag's last distillery, **Van Kleef** (*museumvankleef.nl*), was founded in 1842. Its original location now houses a free museum (closed Monday) with displays including barrels, steam boilers and copper stills, and an atmospherically restored shop stocking Van Kleef's Den Haag–made *jenevers* and *korenwijn* (grain wine) in traditional stoneware bottles, as well as gin and liqueurs; the lush 'secret' garden on the site of the former distilling operations has cellars underneath. On weekends it holds guided tours combined with tastings (*1½ hours; €26.50*) or cocktail tastings (*1¾ hours; €32.50*), accompanied by snacks; book ahead online.

Best Places for...

See p112 for map of locations

€ Budget €€ Midrange €€€ Top End

Eating

Bakeries

Bartine €

20 P113 D6

Stylish boutique bakery with focaccia, sourdoughs, buttery croissants, cardamom 'cruffins' and other sweet treats; you can also stop by for all-day brunch. *8am-4pm*

A La Tarte €

21 P112 A4

Gluten-free and vegan brownies, muffins, cakes, cookies, fruit loaves and sweet pies; many are sugar-free, too. *noon-5pm Fri-Sun, closed Aug*

Wiener Konditorei €

22 P112 D3

Viennese pastry shop and cafe dating from 1934, with Austrian classics including apricot-filled Sacher torte, layered almond-meal *topfentorte*, flaky *apfelstrudel*, custardy *cremeschnitte* and jam-filled berliner doughnuts. *9am-5pm Tue-Sat, 10am-5pm Sun*

Dutch

Dungelmann €

23 P112 C4

Den Haag's most famous *kroketten* (croquettes) and *gehaktballen* (meatballs) since 1861, served on white-bread rolls. *9.30am-6pm Tue, Wed, Fri & Sat, to 9pm Thu, 11.30am-6pm Sun & Mon*

Oma Toos €

24 P113 A4

Oma (grandmother) recipes in this airy space at Scheveningen's harbour include *pannenkoeken* (pancakes), *poffertjes* (mini pancakes) and *stamppot* (mashed veggies with sausage). *10.30am-8.30pm*

Basaal €€

25 P112 D5

Modern Dutch restaurant and wine bar with weekly changing market dishes cooked in a wood-fired oven. *5.30-10.30pm Fri, Sat & Mon, noon-10.30pm Sun*

Seafood

Simonis in de Stad €

26 P112 C5

This 4th-generation fishmonger has pickled herring, smoked eel, shrimp and *kibbeling* (small battered whitefish pieces) to take away, and a restaurant upstairs. *9am-6.30pm Mon-Sat, noon-6.30pm Sun*

Seafood Bar 19 €€

27 P112 D3

Fresh Wadden Sea oysters and mussels served alongside grilled fish, langoustines and lobster in a split-level, herringbone-floored dining room and tree-shaded terrace. *11am-3pm & 5-10pm Tue-Sun*

Wowcrab €€

28 P112 B5

Shellfish bar where North Sea and snow crab, black tiger prawns, lobster, clams and green-shell mussels are doused in spicy Cajun sauce (gloves and seafood crackers provided). *noon-11pm*

Simonis aan de Haven €€

29 P113 A3

At Scheveningen's harbour, Simonis' own fleet delivers the catch to the door, served on piled-high seafood platters with home-baked ciabatta and in dishes such as bouillabaisse. *10am-8pm*

Indonesian

Garuda by Ron Gastrobar €€

30 P112 B3

Four-level restaurant with a ground-floor open kitchen and a top-floor cocktail bar; modern Indonesian street food includes turmeric tempeh tempura and peanut-crusted pork belly. *5-10pm Tue & Wed, noon-3pm & 5-10pm Thu-Sun*

Istana €€

31 P112 C5

Meat, fish and vegetarian *rijsttafels* ('rice tables'; Indonesian banquets) served amid jungle murals, rattan and bamboo lanterns, and palms and other tropical plants. *noon-9.30pm Mon-Sat, 4-10pm Sun*

Waroeng Padang Lapek €€

32 P112 B5

Sumatran restaurant with spicy ginger, lemongrass, garlic and chilli dishes and cooling desserts such as *tjendol* (iced pandan, coconut milk and palm sugar). *noon-9pm Tue-Sun*

Cafes & Brasseries

Onder de Watertoren €

33 P113 D1

Under the 1874 water tower in Oost Duinpark, with pancakes, burgers and ice creams to eat at umbrella-shaded tables or take to the beach. *9.30am-dusk Mar-Oct, weekends only Nov-Feb*

Zebedeüs €€

34 P112 B4

Next to the Grote Kerk, with a chestnut-shaded terrace. Daytime dishes include open sandwiches, soups and toasties, plus cold-pressed juices; there are more elaborate mains at night. *noon-4pm & 5.30-9.30pm*

Walter Benedict €€

35 P112 C2

Sandwiches, snacks and all-day brunches; evening dishes include scallops with samphire and pickled apple or roast celeriac with almond crème and butter-bean purée. *9am-11pm*

Sustainable Dining

Oogst €€

36 P112 C2

Leaves, herbs and vegetables lead the set four-, five- and six-course menus at Oogst (Harvest), with dishes like morel and black-truffle 'cheesecake' (made with cashews) with wild-garlic foam. *6-8.30pm Tue-Sat*

Botanica €€

37 P112 B3

Locally grown fruit and vegetables served from an open kitchen at this restaurant with indoor plants and butterflies on the ceiling, and courtyard-garden tables outside. *10.30am-2pm & 5.30-10.30pm*

Triptyque €€€

38 P112 B6

Menus made from tomato skins set the scene at this Michelin Green Star restaurant by Niven Kunz, where 80% of dishes are vegetarian. *noon-3.30pm Wed, noon-3.30pm & 6-8.30pm Thu-Sat*

Calla's €€€

 P112 C1

Den Haag's only Michelin-star restaurant uses produce from organic, forest-surrounded dune farm Laantje Voorham in refined à la carte and multicourse menus. *noon-2pm & 6.30-8.30pm Tue-Fri, 6.30-8.30pm Sat*

Contemporary

Tommy's & Zuurveen €€

 P112 A3

Lunchtime gourmet open-face sandwiches include poached quail egg with sea urchin; at night, dishes feature unexpected combinations such as pork neck with sea buckthorn. *11am-10pm*

Dekxels €€

41 P112 B2

Stylish exposed-brick and varnished-timber restaurant with a glass-covered, plant-filled terrace; dishes include smoked eel dumplings and brioche katsu chicken. *5-10pm Sun-Thu, to 11pm Fri & Sat*

De Basiliek €€

 P112 D4

Seasonal two- to five-course menus are accompanied by paired wines, while colourful modern art lightens the dark interior at this Korte Houtstraat gem. *noon-3pm & 5.30-10pm Mon-Sat*

Drinking

Wine Bars

Bouzy

43 P112 C1

On buzzing Denneweg, this sun-drenched corner bar has 300 wines and more than 60 varieties of bubbles (many by the glass), alongside snacks including *flammkuchen* (Alsatian-style pizza). *3-11pm Mon-Sat, to 8pm Sun*

De Filosoof

44 P112 B4

Intimate bar with wines from Georgia, Azerbaijan, Moldova and Armenia and small-plate Persian dishes such as leek-filled *ashak* and veal-and-onion *mantu* dumplings. *5-11pm Tue-Thu, 3-11pm Fri & Sat*

Jazz

45 P112 A3

Cafe by day, wine bar by night, with live jazz on Thursday evening and Sunday afternoon and small-producer European wines. *8am-6pm Wed, to 11pm Thu & Fri, to 8pm Sat & Sun*

Cocktails

Gold Bar

46 P112 B3

A 1920s Prohibition-inspired bar accessed by a secret staircase from the Hotel Indigo's lobby in the Netherlands' former gold-reserve bank vault, with heist-themed *jenever*- and gin-based cocktails. *5pm-midnight Wed-Sat*

VaVoom!

47 P112 B5

Tiki bar in Den Haag's main party precinct, with 85 rums available and used in concoctions such as the Jungle Jetsetter (with cherry liqueur and pineapple juice). *4pm-1am Mon-Fri, 2pm-1am Sat & Sun*

Bleyenberg

48 P112 B5

Spread over five levels, including a rooftop bar overlooking the Grote Markt with DJ sets on Friday and Saturday, and basement karaoke, with a seasonal cocktail list. *5pm-1am Wed-Sat*

Zeezicht

49 P113 C1

Beach club on Scheveningen's sand, opposite

the pier, with rattan lounges, fire pit–topped tables and an extensive list of tropical cocktails, including a white rum, blue curacao and strawberry syrup Scheveningen Sunset. *10am-2.30am*

Beer

Rootz

50 P112 B5

Chandelier-lit timber and brick former coach house with over 300 beers (20 on tap) and a large Grote Markt summer terrace. *10am-midnight Sun-Wed, to 1am Thu, to 2am Fri & Sat*

De Paas

51 P112 C5

Huge selection of Dutch, Belgian and international beers, including unusual seasonal brews on its 13 taps, and a floating canal-boat summer terrace. *3pm-midnight Mon-Fri, 2pm-midnight Sat & Sun*

De Zwarte Ruiter

52 P112 B5

The Black Rider is a Grote Markt favourite for its heated terrace, cavernous split-level interior and live acts or DJs on Friday and Saturday nights. *11am-1am Sun-Wed, to 2am Thu-Sat*

Café De Oude Mol

53 P112 B4

An ivy-covered door leads to this pub that sums up Dutch *gezelligheid* (conviviality, cosiness), with live rock on Monday. *5pm-1am Mon-Thu, 4pm-2am Fri & Sat, 4pm-1am Sun*

Coffee

Lola Bikes & Coffee

54 P112 A3

Bike-repair workshop and cafe serving excellent coffee and cake to a host of regulars, with a rear garden and a cycling club welcoming new members. *10am-6pm Mon-Fri, 8.30am-6pm Sat & Sun*

Ief & Ido

55 P112 A6

Beans are roasted on site and served using espresso or V60 methods, with two single-origin options available daily. *10am-5.30pm Wed-Fri, to 5pm Sat & Sun*

Tigershark Coffee

56 P113 B3

Surfer-run Scheveningen cafe with Dutch-roasted beans in espresso tonics and iced lattes alongside vegan chocolate apple cake or pear-and-cardamom crumble, and surfing magazines. *8.30am-3pm Mon-Fri, 9am-4pm Sat & Sun*

Shopping

Books

Bookstor

57 P112 B3

Popular hybrid cafe and secondhand bookstore meeting spot in Het Noordeinde shopping area with chess sets, a bookshelf-lined main room, a rear garden and street-side tables. *8am-8pm*

Boekhandel Douwes

58 P112 D3

Two-level bookshop with several departments, including the Stanley & Livingstone travel section and the English Bookshop with newly released titles. *noon-6pm Mon, 9am-6pm Tue-Fri, 10am-5pm Sat*

Mayflower

59 P112 C4

New, secondhand and antiquarian English bookshop packed floor-to-ceiling with titles;

knowledgeable staff will help you navigate the shelves. *noon-6pm Mon, 10am-6pm Tue-Sat, noon-5pm Sun*

Markets

Borenmarkt

60 P112 C2

Farmers market on Lange Voorhout with seasonal fruit, vegetables and herbs, Dutch cheeses, freshly baked breads, fish, meat and poultry, and condiments such as relishes, sauces and ferments. *10am-6pm Wed May–mid-Sep*

Haagse Antiek en Boekenmarkt

61 P112 C2

High-quality flea market on Lange Voorhout selling antiques, jewellery, furniture, art, ceramics and books at 50-or-so stalls alongside food stalls. *10am-5pm Thu & Sun May–mid-Sep*

De Royal Christmas Fair

62 P112 C3

Festive Lange Voorhout market lit by twinkling lights; 100 stalls sell hot chocolate, mulled wine, and gifts including Delftware, candles and wood carvings. There are also choirs and buskers. *noon-9pm Dec*

De Haagse Markt

63 P112 B6

The Netherlands' largest open-air market: 530 pitches covering over 1300 sq metres, with fresh produce, clothing, fabrics, leather goods and food trucks. *9am-5pm Mon, Wed, Fri & Sat*

Vintage

Ilka

64 P113 D5

Weekly changing collection of women's clothing, with labels such as Sandro, Fillippa K, Burberry and Isabel Marant, and furniture, glassware and mid-century kitchenware. *11am-5pm Wed-Fri, noon-5pm Sat*

Square Eight

65 P112 B5

Street- and skate-wear vintage clothing specialist selling Vans sneakers, Santa Cruz T-shirts, Powell Peralta hoodies and more. *noon-5pm Sun & Mon, 10am-6pm Tue-Sat*

Second Best Selected Treasures

66 P112 A4

Post-1980s secondhand clothing, shoes and accessories for men, women and kids. *noon-5.30pm Tue-Fri, noon-5pm Sat, 1-5pm Sun*

★ WORTH A TRIP

Kinderdijk

Kinderdijk, some 15km southeast of Rotterdam, is a beautiful landscape of waterways and empty marshes. Still in operating condition, 19 historic windmills rise like sentinels above. In summer, tall reeds line the canals, lily pads float on the water and bird calls break the silence.

GETTING THERE
From Rotterdam's Erasmusbrug, Waterbus Line 21 runs direct (*40 minutes*); alternatively, take Line 20 and transfer at Ridderkerk. Check sailing schedules at waterbus.nl. Cycling from Rotterdam takes around an hour.

Scan for practical information.

History

The name Kinderdijk is understood to derive from the tragic St Elizabeth's Day Flood of 1421, when a storm and flood washed a *kind* (child) in a crib up onto the dyke. Since then the area has been a focus of Dutch efforts to claim land from the water. Important types of windmill here include hollow-post mills as well as rotating-cap mills that are among the Netherlands' highest, as they were built to better catch the wind. Kinderdijk was designated a UNESCO World Heritage site in 1997.

Sights & Activities

The Kinderdijk site (*adult/child from €18/6.50, combination ticket with Waterbus from €18/10.25*) encompasses two canals lined by a pedestrian/bicycle path and 19 traditional windmills. Most are used as residences, but two – the 1738-built Nederwaard and the 1630-built Blokweer – are museums providing an insight into the lives of miller families. Short films about the flood, water system and climate management screen aboard the restored 1914-built barge Alles Heeft een Tijd floating outside.

Originally powered by steam, and from 1924 by electricity, the 1868-built Wisboom pumping station, now housing the visitor centre, has displays including an engine-room model. Secondary pumping station De Fabriek screens a film about its

LEOKS/SHUTTERSTOCK ©

history. Learn more about the area's birdlife at the Vogeltheater (Bird Theatre).

The walk or bike ride along the length of the site and back is an easy, flat 5.7km. A hopper boat shuttles along it; the cruiser runs 30-minute summer trips. If you're lucky, some mills will have their sails spinning. Admission includes all activities at the site. The free Kinderdijk app has audio tours.

A glowing spectacle on weekdays during the first full week of September, the windmills are lit by floodlights when the site opens in the evening during Kinderdijk's Illumination Week.

Exploring by Bike

You can bring a bike on the Waterbus for free or rent one close to Kinderdijk. Cycle routes are available on the app. A scenic route follows the Lek river's windmill-dotted southern bank to Bergstoep.

QUICK BREAK

There's a kiosk selling handmade ice creams, a snack bar, and a visitor-centre cafe overlooking the mills that's great for a coffee, sandwich or beer, especially on its terrace (open in fine weather).

★ WORTH A TRIP

Gouda

Gouda's namesake export is renowned, and every Thursday in spring and summer the cheese market is held by the historic *waag* (weighing house). Other attractions include magnificent Sint Janskerk, an excellent museum and a Gothic *Stadhuis* (town hall), all within Gouda's compact, canal-ringed historic centre.

GETTING THERE
Gouda is 25km north-east of Rotterdam, around 1½ hours by bike. Direct trains run frequently from Rotterdam Centraal (*21 minutes; from €5.90*) and from Den Haag (*22 minutes; €6.70*).

Markt

Although cheese has never been commercially made in Gouda, the surrounding dairy farmland established it as a trading centre in the 12th century, and it gained exclusive marketing rights during medieval times, making the name Gouda famous worldwide.

On the town's wedge-shaped Markt costumed volunteers animatedly recreate the tradition of huge wheels of cheese arriving by horse-drawn cart to be unloaded and weighed on the historic scales during the **Gouda Kaasstad** (*10am-12.30pm Thu Apr-Aug*). It's an engaging spectacle, enhanced by regional food stalls and live music.

Today the **Goudse Waag** (*goudsewaag.nl; adult/child €7.50/free*), designed in 1668 by architect Pieter Post, contains a cheese-and-crafts museum with audio tours about the building's history and cheese production and trade.

At the centre of the Markt is the turreted, fairy-tale-like mid-15th-century **Stadhuis** (*town hall; goudastadhuis.nl*). Constructed from sandstone, this Gothic structure is testament to Gouda's wealth from the cloth trade. The beautiful ceremonial rooms are often used for weddings. From mid-December to mid-January it's encircled by an ice-skating rink (*goudseijsbaan.nl*).

Sint Janskerk

Impressive for its size (at 123m, it's the longest church in the country) and its magnificent stained-glass windows, **Sint Janskerk** (*sintjan.com; adult/child €11/free*) had chequered beginnings: previous incarnations of the

CELLI07/SHUTTERSTOCK ©

building burned down with ungodly regularity every 100 years or so from 1361 until the mid-16th century, when the current structure was completed. A free audio guide gives information about the 72 windows, which together form the largest cache of in-situ 16th-century stained glass in the world. It's open Monday to Saturday (Sunday is reserved for services). Check the agenda for concerts.

Museum Gouda

A medieval hospital building houses the town's main **museum** (*museumgouda.nl; adult/child €14/50/free*), closed Monday, has artefacts and artworks related to Gouda and surrounding areas. There's plenty of *Gouds plateel* (glazed earthenware pottery), a collection of paintings by artists of the 19th-century Barbizon and Hague schools, a scale model of Gouda in 1562 and more. The museum also hosts travelling and temporary exhibitions.

QUICK BREAK

On Markt you can enjoy Gouda's other famous delicacy, the *stroopwafel* (caramel-syrup-filled wafers), at 1810-founded **Kamphuisen Siroopwafels** (*siroopwafel fabriek.nl; 45min factory tour from €11.50*), selling oven-fresh *stroopwafels* at its attached shop.

★ WORTH A TRIP

Leiden & the Bollenstreek

Woven by canals lined by 17th-century buildings, Leiden is renowned as Rembrandt's birthplace. Home to the Netherlands' oldest, most prestigious university and a cache of museums within walking distance of each other, it's also a grand gateway to the bulb fields and dunes of the Bollenstreek.

GETTING THERE
Leiden is 36km north of Rotterdam (*37 minutes by train, €8.70*), 25km north of Delft (*24 minutes; €5.90*) and 19km north of Den Haag (*16 minutes; €4.10*), with frequent direct services.

Admire Fine Arts

Leiden's foremost museum for fine art, history and crafts, the **Museum De Lakenhal** (*lakenhal.nl; adult/child €16/free*), closed Monday, occupies a 1640-built former cloth warehouse. Masterpieces among its permanent collection include Rembrandt's *The Spectacles Pedlar*, *The Astronomer* by Gerrit Dou (Rembrandt's first student), *Playing Couple* by Jan Steen and *The Last Judgement* by Lucas van Leyden. Adjoining it, a striking new building hosts temporary exhibitions.

Visit Illuminating Museums

Named in honour of physician, botanist, chemist and University of Leiden teacher Herman Boerhaave (1668–1738), the impressive museum of science and medicine **Rijksmuseum Boerhaave** (*rijksmusumboerhaave.nl; adult/child €15/5.50*) has exhibits profiling major scientific discoveries in the Netherlands. The museum is housed in a 15th-century convent that became the first academic hospital in northern Europe, with a multimedia introduction presented in a recreated anatomical theatre.

The **Rijksmuseum van Oudheden** (*National Museum of Antiquities; adult/child €14/free*), with Greek, Etruscan, Roman and Egyptian artefacts, is especially renowned for its Egyptian halls, which include the reconstructed Temple of Taffeh, mastabas from Saqqara and a room of mummy cases.

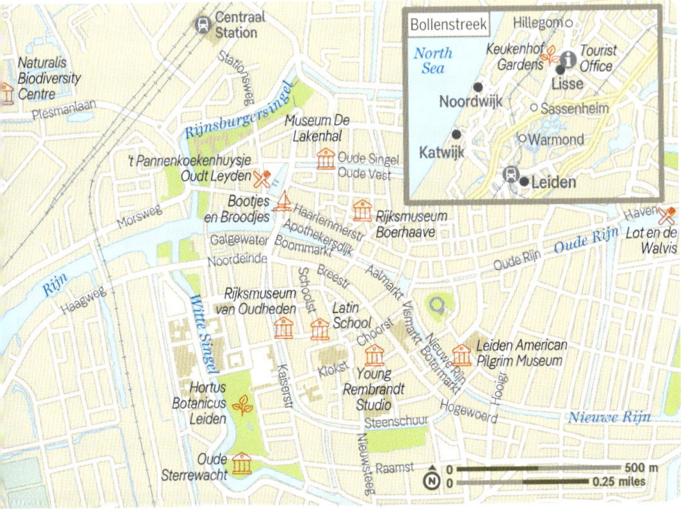

Research institute **Naturalis Biodiversity Centre** (*naturalis.nl; €17*) houses Europe's first T-rex skeleton, named Trix. Sections span botany, geology, entomology (insects), invertebrates, vertebrates and palaeontology (fossils and more) collected by Dutch explorers, archaeologists and scientists all over the globe.

Founded by the university in 1590, the 'living museum' **Hortus Botanicus Leiden** (*hortusleiden.nl; €9*) is one of Europe's oldest botanical gardens; the majority of its collections originate from Southeast and East Asia, including steamy, orchid-filled tropical greenhouses. Admission often includes exhibitions at the 1633-founded **Oude Sterrewacht** (Old Observatory). There are one-hour tours (*€5*) Wednesday to Sunday.

QUICK BREAK

The 1889 old-port warehouse housing all-day hangout **Lot en de Walvis** (*lotendewalvis.nl*) has a waterside terrace; Leiden institution 't Pannenkoekenhuysje **Oudt Leyden** (*oudtleyden.nl*) serves huge Dutch-style pancakes on blue-and-white plates.

KEUKENHOF GARDENS

Stunning **Keukenhof** (*keukenhof.nl*) has springtime displays of seven million bulbs in 800 varieties during its mid-March to mid-May opening season. Tickets, which include special buses from Leiden, are released in autumn.

Follow in Rembrandt's Footsteps

The ninth child of a local miller, Rembrandt van Rijn was born in Leiden in 1606. The Dutch Master is celebrated at the **Young Rembrandt Studio** (*no website; admission free*), closed Mondays. It's set in the 17th-century house at Langebrug 89 where Rembrandt learned his craft between 1606 and 1630, studying in the studio of Jacob van Swanenburgh. Tech wizardry lets you create your own portrait in Rembrandt's distinctive style by holding your face in front of the camera and choosing from its six options (*printing €10*).

The studio is along the 4.5km **Rembrandt Route** walk (*brochure €6.95*), taking in the gabled 1600-built **Latin School** Rembrandt attended from 1616 to 1620.

BORIS STROUJKO/SHUTTERSTOCK ©

Trace the Pilgrims' History

In 1608 a group of Calvinist Protestants split from the Anglican church and left persecution in Nottinghamshire, England. Travelling first to Amsterdam, in Leiden they found a more liberal atmosphere, thanks to the university, like-minded Calvinists and fellow refugees. When England's James I announced in 1618 that he would assume control over the Leiden Calvinists, they travelled to Rotterdam, purchased the *Speedwell* and sailed from Delfshaven (p76) and ultimately to America.

The tiny **Leiden American Pilgrim Museum** (*leidenamericanpilgrimmuseum.org; adult/child €9.50/4.25*), open Thursday, Friday and Saturday afternoons, is a fascinating restoration of a house occupied around 1610 by the soon-to-be Pilgrims. The house itself dates from 1365–70 (check out the original 14th-century floor tiles), but the furnishings are from the Pilgrims' period. It co-created Leiden's **Pilgrim Route** walking tour; a route brochure (*€0.95*) is available at Leiden's **tourist office** opposite Centraal Station.

Cruise Leiden's Waterways

Within its city centre, Leiden has 28km of canals spanned by 88 bridges that are idyllic for exploring by boat for a unique perspective on its historic architecture. Numerous companies rent boats to set sail under your own steam. Boats typically accommodate six people and don't require a boat licence (you're provided with instructions, rules and route information). Rates start at around €125 for two hours. Try **Bootjes en Broodjes** (*bootjesenbroodjes.nl*).

If you'd rather sit back with someone else at the helm, Bootjes en Broodjes is also among the Leiden operators offering guided canal cruises (*50-minute cruise adult/child €12.50/7.50*) in open-topped electric boats that are covered and heated in winter.

LEIDEN'S UNIVERSITY

The Netherlands' oldest university, **Universiteit Leiden** (*universiteitleiden.nl*), was a gift to Leiden from William the Silent in 1575 for withstanding two Spanish sieges in 1573 and 1574. Illustrious professors who have taught here include Einstein, and scientists' collections have contributed to the city's concentration of museums. The campus is a mix of modern and historic buildings that are scattered around town.

Cycle the Bollenstreek: Bulb Fields Tour

Pick up wheels in Leiden (rental outlets abound) for a spectacular half-day loop through fragrant bulb fields that are ablaze with colourful tulips, jonquils, daffodils and hyacinths in spring (around mid-March to mid-May), and blooms such as dahlias, asters and sunflowers in late summer (mid-August to mid-October), before returning via forest and wildflower-strewn coastal dunes.

START	END	LENGTH
Molen De Valk (train Leiden Centraal)	Vlot Grand Café (train Leiden Centraal)	51km; 4 hours

1 Windmill Museum

Built in 1743, Leiden's landmark tower windmill, **Molen De Valk** (*molenmuseumdevalk.nl; adult/child €6/3*), now contains a museum; the last grain was ground here in the 1960s.

2 Flower Farm

North of summer swimming lake Klinkenbergerplas, you'll enter the bulb fields at Sassenheim, along mid-April's 42km-long Bloemencorso (Flower Parade) route. Just north, **De Tulperij** (*detulperij.nl; 1hr tours adult/child from €7.95/4.50*) has farm tours, show gardens and pick-your-own flowers in season.

3 'Cathedral of the Bollenstreek'

A quick spin north-east brings you to Lisse's beautiful 1900-built church **Sint Agathakerk** (*willibrordusbollenstreek.nl*), co-funded by local bulb growers and featuring flower motifs.

4 Tulip Museum

Just north on Heereweg is the **Museum de Zwarte Tulp** (*Museum of the Black Tulip; museumdezwartetulp.nl; adult/child €10/5*); displays include mythical black tulips that helped fuel Tulipmania in 1636.

5 Tulip Barn

Take Stationweg north-east, passing Kasteel Keukenhof – you can visit the forest, grounds and art gallery LAM (*lammuseum.nl; adult/child €7.50/5*), though not the castle itself, and world-famous Keukenhof Gardens (p138) before cycling through bulb fields that burst into colour in spring. **The Tulip Barn** (*thetulipbarn.com; €8.50/3.50*) grows upwards of 750,000 tulips in 175 varieties and has a greenhouse cafe.

6 Tulip Experience

Cycle north-west to De Zilk and take Zilkerbinnenweg south-west to the **Tulip Experience** (*tulipexperienceamsterdam.nl; adult/child €11/6.50*). Its show garden has one million colourful tulips in 700 varieties; there's a museum and indoor picking barn.

7 Viewing Platform

Ride south on Delfweg and north-west on Houtvesterslaan. Climb the wooden boardwalk-like staircase to the 14m-high **Uitkijkpunt Tespelduyn** (*tespelduyn.nl; admission free*) for fantastic views of the colour-streaked fields below (and Den Haag beyond).

8 Canalside Cafe

Cycle north to Ruigenhoek and swing west through shady forest into the Noordduinen dune system. Parallelling the coastal Strand Noordwijk south, look for dune violets, orange-berried sea buckthorn and pink-flowering pyramidal orchids. At Katwijk aan Zee, head south-east along Zeeweg and Provincialeweg to return to Leiden and enjoy a beer on the floating terrace at **Vlot Grand Café** (*vlotleiden.nl*).

Rotterdam Toolkit

Markthal (p44)

CHRISTIAN MUELLER/SHUTTERSTOCK ©

Family Travel

Rotterdam offers plenty of activities for families travelling with children. There are parks for little ones to play in, loads of museums with kid-friendly activities, and an exciting array of boats and trams to board.

Is Rotterdam Good for Kids?

The entire region is brilliant to explore as a family. Along with Rotterdam's attractions (including the zoo, miniature world, urban surfing), it's easy to visit storybook-like old Dutch cities, Den Haag's fun amusement park, and windmills and beaches. The famous Dutch tolerance extends to children, and locals are exceptionally welcoming towards them (and parents too).

BY BIKE

Dutch kids are raised on *fietsen* (bicycles). Most bike-rental shops carry trailers, child and baby seats and kid-sized bikes. In summer it's best to book pre-arrival. Not all rental outlets offer helmets (for any age), so consider bringing your own.

Sightseeing

Admission rates for children vary. Some museums are free to under-18s, while others only offer free or reduced admission to under-17s, under-12s or even younger kids; some only provide free entry to kids under four, five or six. Attractions aimed specifically at kids tend to charge a flat admission rate. Take advantage of family tickets where available.

Sleeping

Hotels rarely have a 'no kids' rule. Most have extra beds (at minimal cost) or baby cots (free) on request.

Public Transport

Under-fours travel free; children aged four to 11 are eligible for reduced-price tickets.

Eating

All but the most formal restaurants welcome children. Kids' menus are common and often include deep-fried treats. You can ask for high chairs and crayons in many restaurants. Pancake restaurants are popular throughout the Netherlands.

Accommodation

Accommodation options are limited; book well ahead, especially if you're travelling here between April and September, the region's high season.

Where to stay if you love...

Local Atmosphere, Creative Energy

Footsteps from Rotterdam Centraal Station, **Noord (p58)** has an up-and-coming energy, especially around the Hofbogen viaduct, with lots of eating and drinking choices (though limited accommodation).

We love to stay in...

Centrum (p32)

Most places to stay in Rotterdam are found here, and that's no surprise: Centrum is Rotterdam's beating heart, with a diverse array of must-see museums, activities from boat tours to urban surfing, the city's best concentration of eating, drinking, shopping and nightlife, and proximity to transport (including watertaxis, an exhilarating way to get around).

Cool Hotels, Water views

High-rise hotels in **Zuid (p84)** have glittering skyline views, while other great options include the Holland America Line's historic HQ and one of its steam liners, too.

Quiet Areas, Quirky Options

Sprawling **West (p68)** spans a central pocket from lively Nieuwe Binnenweg to leafy residential streets, pretty port Delfshaven and a panoramic two-room hotel atop the Euromast.

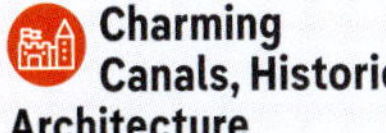

Charming Canals, Historic Architecture

A short train ride from Rotterdam, delightful **Delft (p96)** retains its 17th-century streetscapes from Vermeer's time and is especially lovely without day-tripping crowds after dark.

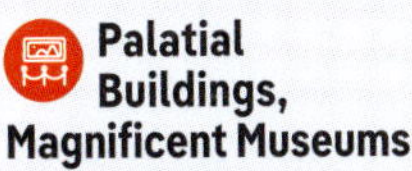

Palatial Buildings, Magnificent Museums

Also an easy train trip from Rotterdam, the Netherlands' royal and governmental seat **Den Haag (p110)** has a vibrant city centre, beautiful parks and the sandy Scheveningen beach.

HOW MUCH FOR A NIGHT IN

Hostel dorm bed from **€35**

Midrange boutique hotel from **€120**

Luxury city centre hotel from **€200**

 Food, Drink & Nightlife

Allergies & Intolerances

People with allergies and intolerances will generally have no problems in Rotterdam and surrounds (an exception is high-end establishments offering 'surprise', no-choice menus); check when you book and communicate your requirements clearly with waitstaff to be sure.

HOW TO SAY

I'm allergic to... Ik ben allergisch voor...
...peanuts ...pindas
...nuts ...noten
...seafood ...zeevruchten
...eggs ...eieren
...milk ...melk
...gluten ...gluten

HOW TO ASK...

Is this gluten-free?
Is dit glutenvrij?
Does this contain nuts?
Zitten hier noten in?
Is there a vegan option?
Is er een veganistische optie?

COFFEESHOPS & CAFES

In the Netherlands it's crucial to know the difference between a coffeeshop (marijuana-smoking cafe), a coffee shop (*koffiehuis*; a specialist espresso bar serving craft coffee) and a *café* (pub). A coffeeshop may serve coffee (never alcohol), but its focus is cannabis and hash. Smoking (any substance) is banned by law in *cafés*.

 Vegetarians & Vegans

The Netherlands is a plant-based cuisine pioneer, and a quarter of main meals eaten here are vegetarian. Vegetarians and vegans will find options in all price categories. Many cafes and restaurants are exclusively vegetarian or completely vegan; most others usually have vegetarian (and often vegan) dishes or set menus available.

HOW TO... Pay the Bill

In many establishments waitstaff will ask upfront if you would like separate bills (*aparte rekening*) or one (*één rekening*). Requesting separate bills from the outset considerably expedites settling up later.

After your meal you can ask for '*De rekening alstublieft.*' ('The bill please.')

Tipping is customary but not obligatory. Check the bill to see if the service charge is already included. Typically, people round up the bill or leave a small tip of around 5%; a 10% tip is considered generous. State the amount you want to pay, including the tip, as you hand your payment to your server.

FROM LEFT: RTSTUDIO/SHUTTERSTOCK ©, GRAJA/SHUTTERSTOCK ©, ANDREI KUZMIK/SHUTTERSTOCK ©

PRICE RANGES

The following price categories refer to the cost of a main course:

€ less than €12

€€ €12–25

€€€ more than €25

OPENING HOURS

Cafes and bars Hours vary, but generally noon to 1am Sunday to Thursday, to 3am Friday and Saturday

Restaurants 11am to 2.30pm and 6pm to 10pm

Going Out

Where to go

Rotterdam's cafes, cocktail bars, microbreweries and pubs – many with outdoor seating in summer – are scattered across various neighbourhoods. Witte de Withstraat in Centrum is the main bar and nightlife street.

Borrel Literally meaning 'drink', socially *borrel* is an informal gathering for drinks, invariably with *borrelhapjes* (bar snacks) such as *bitterballen* (small croquettes).

Beer Seen as the perfect companion for time spent with friends in the sun or out partying till the small hours. Traditionally clear, crisp lager (or Pilsner), beer is served cool and topped by a head of froth. *Een bier or een pils* will get you a normal glass; *een kleintje pils* is a small glass and *een fluitje* is a tall, thin glass – perfect for multiple refills.

Entertainment Music dominates, with plentiful festivals and venues. Many live-music stages resist being confined to one genre, programming everything from jazz to rock, reggae to R&B.

HOW MUCH FOR A

Coffee €3.50

Stroopwafel €2.50

Friet (fries) €4

Sandwich €7–12

Fluitje (22cL glass) of beer €4.50

Bitterballen (six croquettes) €5

Dinner for two from €40

Cocktail €9.50

LGBTIQ+ Travellers

Inclusivity and diversity are embraced in Rotterdam and across the Netherlands – the world's first country to legalise same-sex marriage, in 2001.

Pride in Rotterdam

Rotterdam's Pride celebrations are some of the latest in Europe's annual calendar, taking place in the last week of September each year and bringing the local LGBTIQ+ community and allies together along with visitors. Although the Pride foundation ran into financial difficulties, other local organisations stepped into the breach to ensure activities in 2024; going forward, expect Pride Week activities and events to include anything from film screenings to sports sessions, cooking workshops, ballroom dancing classes, gin and tonic walking/cycling/running courses, drag brunches, and a Pride Walk, as well as plenty of parties. Check the latest at openrotterdam.nl.

For Pride celebrations on a global scale, circle 25 July to 8 August 2026, when nearby Amsterdam commemorates 25 years of marriage equality during World Pride (worldpride.amsterdam).

DEN HAAG'S PRIDE

Held in mid-May, Den Haag's Pride (*pridethehague.nl*) was revived in 2024, with plans to grow. Events include a Pride Walk, and take place in the city and at the beach.

OUR PICKS

Best LGBTIQ+ Drinking & Nightlife

Rotterdam venues cluster around Westblaak:

Ferry DJs Thursday to Monday, plus parties.

Bar Loge 90 Leopard-print wallpaper, chandeliers and theme nights.

Bonaparte Regular drag shows.

Cafe Strano Intimate late-night bar.

KeerWeer Dancing until dawn.

Den Haag's oldest gay bar, **De Vink**, dates from the 60s; **'t Achterom** is a contemporary favourite.

QUEER AAN ZEE

Scan this QR code for details of meet-ups, events, activities, venues and other tips for tapping into Den Haag's scene.

Resources

• **en.rotterdam.info/nightlife/gay-friendly-rotterdam** Resources from Rotterdam's tourism authority • **essm.stichtinghumanitas.org** Part of the Humanitas Foundation and an organiser of Rotterdam's Pride celebrations • **queerfest.nl** Presents festivities as part of Rotterdam's Pride Week • **denhaag.com/nl/lhbtiq-in-den-haag** Information from Den Haag's tourism authority • **dwhdelft.nl/en** Delft's independent LGBTIQ+ association

Health & Safe Travel

Rotterdam and the wider region are generally extremely safe so long as you stay alert and take common-sense precautions.

TAP WATER

The Netherlands' tap water is clean, drinkable and well filtered. Bring a water bottle to keep hydrated. Drinking fountains are widely available across parks, campgrounds, tourist areas and transport hubs. In restaurants, feel free to ask for *kraanwater* (tap water), which is usually free of charge.

Insurance

Travel insurance is vital. Make sure your policy covers scenarios such as an accident requiring an emergency flight home, and check whether it will make payments directly to providers or reimburse you later for overseas health expenditures. If you're an EU citizen, a European Health Insurance Card (EHIC) covers you for medically necessary care, but not nonemergencies or emergency repatriation. Citizens of other countries should check if their country has a reciprocal arrangement with the Netherlands.

Carry ID

By law, police and regulatory bodies can request proof of ID; always carry it with you.

Drugs

Be aware that cannabis is illegal in the Netherlands: while small quantities (up to 5g) are generally tolerated by authorities, it's policed differently by municipalities, and some areas enforce cannabis -smoking bans in public places. (Government policies are also apt to change.) Never buy any drugs on the street – fatalities can and do occur.

PHARMACIES

For minor illnesses or injuries an *apotheek* (pharmacy) can give valuable advice, sell over-the-counter medication and point you to more specialised help if required.

QUICK INFO

Lock Bicycles

Always lock bicycles, preferably in busy areas, or find a guarded bike park.

Pickpockets

Watch belongings in crowds; pickpockets frequent busy transport hubs and landmarks.

Bike Lanes

Look extra-carefully both ways before crossing bike lanes.

Responsible Travel

Follow these tips to leave a lighter footprint, support local and have a positive impact on communities.

Emissions-free Public Transport

Taking public transport in Rotterdam helps reduce your carbon footprint. The city's operator, RET, uses 100% renewable energy, running exclusively on 'green power' generated in the Netherlands from 2024 and transitioning to a 100% emissions-free bus fleet by 2030. Watertaxi Rotterdam added the first hydrogen-powered watertaxi to its fleet in 2022, and now over a quarter run on renewable energy; it's planning for an emission-free fleet by 2030.

Circular Economy

According to Arcadis' rankings, Rotterdam is the world's second most sustainable city (after Amsterdam). The Netherlands is aiming for a fully circular economy by 2050, reusing, repairing and recycling materials to eliminate waste

OUR PICK

Waste-free Savings

Pick up bargain-priced unsold items at merchants such as bakeries via the app Too Good to Go (*toogoodtogo.nl*), which helps prevent food waste.

Eco Dining

Chefs across Rotterdam and its surrounds champion sustainable dining. Local, seasonal ingredients grace menus everywhere. Rotterdam's **NOTK** (p92) mills its own bread and churns its own butter, while **Putaine** (p92), on the Rijnhaven's FOR (Floating Office Rotterdam), makes its own ferments and uses Delfshaven-landed seafood. At Den Haag's **Triptyque** (p128), even the menus are made from tomato skins, while **Calla's** (p129) uses organic dune-farm produce.

Resources

• **en.rotterdam.info/sustainable-rotterdam** Loads of links to the city's sustainable options • **nederlandfietsland.nl** Route planner for the Netherlands' cycling-path network

GREENING THE CITY

Emerging green spaces include the Rijnhaven's **floating parks** (p89), the Hofbogenpark by the **Luchtpark Hofbogen** (p63) and the Schieblock's rooftop urban farm and cafe **Teds** (p53), and **Blaakpark**, the Netherlands' largest city-centre park, opening in 2027.

Sustainable Shopping

Rotterdam's number-one stop for sustainable shopping is **De Groene Passage** (p56), a 'green passage' with only sustainable small businesses (design, natural beauty, groceries, vegan dining and cocktails). Elsewhere, chocolate manufacturer **De Bonte Koe** (p83) uses sustainably sourced ingredients, solar power, recycled packaging and emission-free deliveries.

Bags and raincoats made by **Susan BIJL** (p83) use recycled fabrics made from plastic bottles. Vintage shops include **CENO** (p67) for quality natural-fibre clothing and **Daily Sneaker Steals** (p83) for cool second-hand kicks. Hunt through Delft's weekly summer **Antickmarkt** (p109), with over 100 stalls selling delftware, Dutch antiques and art, for charming souvenirs.

EMBRACE CYCLING CULTURE

A way of life in the Netherlands, cycling is the ultimate eco-friendly way to get around, with superb city- and countrywide infrastructure. Rentals are readily available; check listnride.com (you can filter for shops) or use the Donkey Republic app (*donkey.bike*).

Climate Change & Travel

It's impossible to ignore the impact we have when travelling; Lonely Planet urges all travellers to engage with their travel carbon footprint, which will mainly come from air travel. While there often isn't an alternative, travellers can look to minimise the number of flights they take, opt for newer aircrafts and use cleaner ground transport, such as trains. One proposed solution—purchasing carbon offsets—unfortunately does not cancel out the impact of individual flights. While most destinations will depend on air travel for the foreseeable future, for now, pursuing ground-based travel where possible is the best course of action.

The **UN carbon footprint calculator** shows how flying impacts a household's emissions.

The **ICAO's Carbon Emissions Calculator** allows visitors to analyse the CO_2 generated by point-to-point journeys.

Accessible Travel

Public Transport

All Rotterdam train and metro stations have wheelchair ramps, lifts and escalators; most train stations and some metro stations have accessible toilets. Bus routes, tram lines and stops with a wheelchair sticker are wheelchair accessible. Buses have low boarding platforms; some bus and tram stops also have level-floor boarding.

Dining Out

Restaurants tend to be on ground floors, ie street level (*begane grond*; BG) – the 1st floor (*eerste verdieping*) is the floor above. Even ground-floor restaurants still sometimes have a few steps. Restaurant bathrooms aren't always wheelchair accessible or fitted with rails.

POTENTIAL HAZARDS

Cobblestone streets and squares, such as those in towns Delft and Gouda, can be rough for wheelchairs and for travellers with vision impairment. Canals and waterways aren't fenced or guarded by barriers.

Airports

Reduced Mobility Rights (reducedmobility.eu) is a resource on accessibility in the EU, including passengers' rights and airline and airport information. Schiphol Airport's website (*schiphol.nl*) also has information on passenger assistance for those with reduced mobility.

Exhibitions at the city's maritime museum, the **Maritiem Museum Rotterdam** (p49), can be accessed by visitors with reduced mobility, with wheelchair accessibility and lifts (elevators), a ground-floor accessible toilet, and a wheelchair available for visitors. From the museum building, the harbourside quays are accessible (though the ships and cranes aren't). Guide dogs are welcomed. Hidden Disabilities Sunflower lanyards are recognised by staff, who offer assistance. Children's exhibits are designed to meet the approval of the Netherlands Foundation for Disabled Children.

ACCESSIBLE BULB-FIELDS CYCLING

In the Bollenstreek, **Lemonbike** (*lemonbike.nl*) rents lightweight electric special-needs single and tandem bicycles with a swivel seat, fixed-seat wheelchair bikes, wheelchair transport bikes, and beach wheelchairs.

Resources

- **Accessible Travel Netherlands** (*accessibletravelnl.com*) Hotel bookings, transport, accessible tours, activities and tailored itineraries; can organise mobility-equipment rental too.

Nuts & Bolts

Opening Hours

Hours can vary seasonally, often decreasing during the low season.

Banks 9am–4pm Monday to Friday, some Saturday morning

Cafes and bars Hours often vary

General business hours 8.30am–5pm Monday to Friday

Museums 10am or 11am–5pm daily, most close Monday

Restaurants noon–2.30pm and 6–10pm

Shops 11am–7pm Monday, 10am–7pm Tuesday to Thursday, 10am–9pm Friday, 10am–7pm Saturday, noon–7pm Sunday

Supermarkets 8am–8pm

QUICK INFO

Time zone Central European Time (GMT/UTC plus one hour)

City calling code 010

Emergency number 112

Population 1.02 million

ELECTRICITY

230V/50Hz

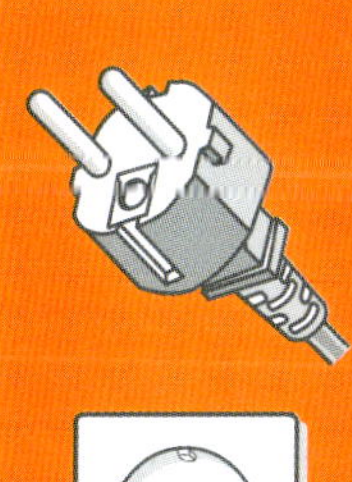

Type F
230V/50Hz

Public Toilets

Convenient public toilet locations include the upper floor of Rotterdam Centraal Station and the centrally located Bijenkorf department store. The app HogeNood (High Need; *www.hogenood.nu*) maps the nearest toilets based on your location, listing facilities in fast-food stores, department stores, public buildings, tourist offices and pubs.

Public Holidays

Nieuwjaarsdag (New Year's Day) 1 January

Eerste Paasdag Easter Sunday, March/April

Tweede Paasdag Easter Monday, March/April

Koningsdag (King's Day) 27 April (26 April if the 27th is a Sunday)

Bevrijdingsdag (Liberation Day) 5 May; many people treat Dodenherdenking (Remembrance Day; 4 May) as a day off

Hemelvaartsdag (Ascension Day) Fortieth day after Easter Sunday

Eerste Pinksterdag (Whit Sunday; Pentecost) Fiftieth day after Easter Sunday

Tweede Pinksterdag (Whit Monday) Fiftieth day after Easter Monday

Eerste Kerstdag (Christmas Day) 25 December

Tweede Kerstdag ('Second Christmas', aka Boxing Day) 26 December

Open
Open

Gesloten
Closed

Language

Dutch Basics

Hello.
Dag/Hallo.
dakh/ha·loh

Goodbye.
Dag.
dakh

Yes.
Ja.
yaa

No.
Nee.
ney

Please.
Alstublieft. (pol)
po al·stew·bleeft
Alsjeblieft. (inf)
a·shuh·bleeft

Thank you.
Dank u/je. (pol/inf)
dangk ew/yuh

Excuse me.
Excuseer mij.
eks·kew·zeyr mey

Sorry.
Sorry.
so.ree

Fast Phrases

How are you?
Hoe gaat het met u/jou? (pol/inf). *hoo khaat huht met ew/yaw*

Fine. And you?
Goed. En met u/jou? (pol/inf). *khoot en met ew/yaw*

Do you speak English?
Spreekt u Engels? *spreykt ew eng·uhls*

Please bring the bill.
Mag ik de rekening alstublieft? *makh ik duh rey·ku-h·ning al·stew·bleeft*

How much is it?
Hoeveel kost het? *hoo·veyl kost huht*

Where's the...?
Waar is ...? *waar is...*

What time is it?
Hoe laat is het? *hoo laat is huht*

It's (10) o'clock.
Het is (tien) uur. *huht is (teen) ewr*

Half past (10). **Half (elf).** *half (elf)* (lit: half eleven)

in the morning. **'s ochtends.** *sokh·tuhns*

in the afternoon. **'s middags.** *smi·dakhs*

in the evening. **'s middags.** *saa·vonts*

yesterday. **gisteren.** *khis·tuh·ruhn*

tomorrow. **morgen.** *mor·khuhn*

Numbers

één eyn

twee twey

drie dree

vier veer

vijf veyf

Good to Know

Slang in a foreign language is tricky, but listen out for these words and phrases and even have a go at using them.

joe (*yo*) is slang for 'hello', 'goodbye' and getting attention; **groetjes** (*khroot-yes*) or 'greetings' is also common.

pá'dag (*dakh*) is 'goodbye' for for everyday interactions.

tjuus (*choos*) is 'goodbye' but a little cute.

proost (*prohst*) is 'cheers' (toasting).

lekker (*leh-kur*) is a mustlearn! Used for 'delicious', 'cool', 'awesome' – food, fashion, places etc.

strand (*strahnd*) is 'beach'.

fiets (*feets*) is 'bicycle'.

EMERGENCIES

Help! **Help!** *help*

Call a doctor!
Bel een dokter!
bel uhn dok·tuhr

Call the police!
Bel de politie!
bel duh poh·leet·see

I'm lost.
Ik ben verdwaald.
ik ben vuhr·dwaalt

I'm sick.
Ik ben ziek.
ik ben zeek

Food Words

Bitterballen Deep-fried ragout balls with dipping mustard

Patatje Frites in cone shaped paper wrapping topped with ketchup and/or mayo

Pannenkoeken Thin pancakes with sweet or savoury toppings

Poffertjes Puffy minipan-cakes layered with butter and powdered sugar

Kroket Deep-fried meat ragout fast-food snack eaten in a bun

Distinctive Sounds

Note that öy is pronounced as the 'er y' (without the 'r') in 'her year', and kh is a throaty sound, similar to the 'ch' in the Scottish loch.

TRANSPORT & DIRECTIONS

How far is it? **Hoe ver is het?** *hoo ver is huht*

What's the address? **Wat is het adres?** *wat is huht a·dres*

Can you show me (on the map)? **Kunt u het mij tonen (op d ekaart)?** *kunt ew huht mey toh·nuhn (op duh kaart)*

A ticket to...please. **Een kaartje naar...graag.** *uhn kaar·chuh naar...khraakh*

Please take me to... **Breng me alstublieft naar...** *breng muh al·stew·bleeft naar...*

zes zes

zeven zey·vuhn

acht akht

negen ney·khuhn

tien teen

Index

Sights p000 Map pages **p000**

See also separate subindexes for:
Eating p158
Drinking p159
Shopping p159

Eating

Drinking

Shopping

Send Us Your Feedback

We love to hear from travellers – your comments help make our books better. We read every word, and we guarantee that your feedback goes straight to the authors. Visit lonelyplanet.com/contact to submit your updates and suggestions.

Note: We may edit, reproduce and incorporate your comments in Lonely Planet products such as guidebooks, websites and digital products, so let us know if you are happy to have your name acknowledged. For a copy of our privacy policy visit lonelyplanet.com/legal.

Acknowledgements

Cover photograph: Markthal. Walter Bibikow/AWL Images ©

"Horn of Plenty" by Arno Coenen & Iris Roskam, in collaboration with Mothership

Back photograph: Cube houses in Rotterdam. pixelshop/ Shutterstock ©

THIS BOOK

Destination Editor
Sandie Kestell

Cartographer
Rachel Imeson

Production Editor
Ursula O'Sullivan-Dale

Book Designer
Dominic Allen

Assisting Editors
Maja Vatrić, Jennifer McCann, Charlotte Orr, Kate Matthews

Cover Researcher
Hannah Blackie

Thanks to
Alison Killilea, Sarah Bailey, Ronan Abayawickrema

Published by Lonely Planet Global Limited

2nd edition – Jul 2025

ISBN 978 1 78868 099 8

10 9 8 7 6 5 4 3 2 1

Printed in China